Miscellaneous
Musings

Miscellaneous Musings

Reg M. Reynolds

To order additional copies of this book, contact:
Xlibris
1-888-795-4274
www.Xlibris.com
Orders@Xlibris.com
788820

CONTENTS

CHAPTER 1

An Introduction to Hypnosis

During a past summer, a friend of mine was travelling with his wife, by car, through the province of Saskatchewan when they found themselves driving through a number of small towns with native Canadian names. In most cases, they could agree on how to pronounce the names of these small towns; but eventually they came to one small town on which they couldn't agree. So they pulled into a little store, and got out and went in, and he said to the girl at the counter, "Would you pronounce the name of this place for us, very slowly?" And she said, "D-A-I-R-Y Q-U-E-E-N." Now, there is a lot of information to cover in even this brief introduction to hypnosis, so you may want to ... attend very carefully to what I have to say.[1]

During this introduction to hypnosis, I will be taking you on a magical mystery tour de force, and it stands to reason that some of the information that I present will be of less interest to your conscious mind then to your unconscious ... mind, I want to assure you that it is all right for you to ... only attend to those parts which are of most interest to your conscious mind. And rest ... assured that ... your unconscious ... mind ... will hear and ... remember everything that I tell you, and ... keep it available for you to ... use in your practice of hypnosis now ... and in the future.

A long time ago, in a land far away, human nature was divided into two parts, an executive part called a God and a follower part

---

1   ... indicates a very brief pause, a "stutter step" as it were, to provide emphasis to whatever follows immediately.

called a man. Neither part was conscious. The man simply lived his life without thinking about it, and the God-part spoke to him from time to time, as one person to another, to tell him what to do. You may wonder how that could be.

In the dawn of history, mankind did not have a mental language. The pictogram language which we associate with Cro-Magnon man had consisted of pictures of visual events familiar to the artists, in contrast to our own writing which is primarily designed to give the reader information about something that he does not already know. Midway between these two kinds of writing were the hieroglyphs, the term meaning "the writing of the Gods," and the more widely used cuneiform writing with its wedge-shaped characters.

Most of the cuneiform literature is in the form of receipts or inventories, i.e., the subject matter was quite down-to-earth. But then a dramatic change occurred. About 1200 B.C., the king of Assyria had a stone altar made that was dramatically different from anything that had preceded it since the beginning of time. In the days of Hammurabi, for example, the king was often pictured as standing and listening intently to a very present God. Suddenly, in the carving on the face of this stone altar erected by the king of Assyria, the king is shown twice, first as he approaches the throne of his God, and then as he kneels before it, and the throne before which he kneels is empty. No king before in history is ever shown as kneeling; no scene before in history indicates an absent God.

In fact, it wasn't until about this time in history that language had evolved to the point where man could consciously have a conversation with himself, and the Gods began to withdraw from his company and to make their home in heaven; and winged beings, angels (or genies, as the Assyrians called them) began to appear as intermediaries or messengers between the absent Gods and their forlorn followers. In addition, demons began to appear and needed to be defended against, and a priestly caste arose. In Persia, they were known as the Magi, or Magicians.

Now when Jesus was born in Bethlehem of Judea in the days of Herod the King, behold, there came wise men from the east to

Jerusalem, saying, "Where is he that is born King of the Jews? For we have seen his star in the east, and are come to worship him." From these few sentences in St. Matthew, a whole legend developed during the Middle Ages. The wise men became three in number, were promoted to kings, and finally, during the sixth century acquired the names of Melchior, Gaspar, and Balthazar which, in Syriac tradition, are Persian and associated with Persian religious history.

The term "magic" is derived from the Greek "mageia," meaning the occult learning and practices of the Persian Magi. This magic was not merely an irrational substitute for a not-yet-developed science; it was an active attempt at mastery of a none-too-friendly world; and as long as the Persian empire lasted, i.e., well into the middle ages, the wisdom of the Magi was held in high esteem. Their magic was even given official recognition by the developing Christian church. After all, wasn't it the Magi who, through their astrology, had been among the first to discover Christ.

It has been said that the history of hypnosis runs back to antiquity (Coppolino, 1965) when it was used by the Persian Magi, for example, as a treatment for possession by evil spirits and by the fakirs of India as a form of anaesthesia. "The Druids, at the beginning of the Christian Era, were versatile in their use of hypnosis, and music was one of their chief ways of inducing this so-called "magical sleep" (Williams, p.6), and some of the "fairy" lullabies of Scotland and Ireland can be traced to these same sources. In Biblical times, we read about the laying on of hands for the healing of the sick, a practice which was carried on by kings and emperors during the middle ages, and called the Royal Touch. In the sixteenth century, Paracelsus wrote in part, "Man possesses a hidden power which may be, in a way, compared to a magnet, for by his power, man attracts the surrounding chaos, and this magnetism comes down from the stars." (quoted in Coppolino, p.4).

It wasn't until some two hundred years later, however, that Frederich Anton Mesmer introduced us to the term "animal magnetism" as an explanation for the powerful affects *which he was able to produce* through what is now known as hypnosis. Shortly after being graduated with a medical degree from the University of Vienna in 1766, Mesmer wrote: "I believe that health is based on a fluidum (and) that this fluid comes from magnets and astral bodies." At the time, a contemporary of Mesmer's, one Father Gasner, was achieving considerable success as an exorcist, literally scaring the devil out of his patients; Mesmer wrote that "What this clerical gentleman is doing is superstition; what I am doing is science. I'm talking about magnetism, and magnetism is something every scientist can know something about." In fact, he spent a great deal of his time conducting scientific experiments in an attempt to demonstrate the validity of his theories; and when he did get around to putting his theories into practice, Mesmerism soon became a household word, and patients literally flocked to his door begging to be cured.

Within the scientific community, however, not everyone was willing to accept the scientific validity of "Mesmerism." In 1784, at the request of the French Academy of Medicine, King Louis XVI, the last king of France before the fall of the monarchy during the French Revolution, appointed a committee of physicians and scientists to investigate Mesmer's work. The committee was composed of four doctors and five laymen, including Benjamin Franklin, the French chemist Lavoisier, and one Joseph Guillotine, later famous as the inventor of that ingenious device though which so many of the aristocracy were to lose their heads. In due time, they passed a resolution branding mesmerism as sheer imagination; and, at least within the scientific community, mesmerism fell into disrepute.

Still, there had been some who had been impressed by the power of the procedures that Mesmer had used, if not by the pre-psychological theories with which he had attempted to explain them. During the eighteen hundreds, hypnosis continued to be used as an anaesthetic in many major operations. In 1842, for example, an English surgeon by the name of Ward successfully removed a leg at the thigh under hypnosis, and between 1845 and 1851 a Dr. James Esdaile performed approximately 300 major operations in India, using hypnosis as the only anaesthetic. In 1846, however, ether was discovered, closely followed by chloroform; and from then until the Second World War, chemo-anaesthesia was used almost exclusively.

In the mid-eighteen hundreds, the English physician, James Braid, suggested that the hypnotic effects that Mesmer had produced with such regularity could be explained solely on the basis of concentrated attention. That is, he proposed that hypnotic phenomena were both genuine and important, but that they are essentially psychological in nature. The same conclusion was arrived at independently in France by an unassuming country doctor from the small town of Nancy, Ambroise Liebeault, and by the professor of medicine from Strasbourg, Hippolyte Bernheim, who championed his views; and Bernheim soon succeeded in drawing world wide attention to the importance of mental therapeutics based on verbal suggestion.

Hypnotic therapy in the Nancy tradition, however, consisted essentially of induction of a state of heightened suggestibility followed by verbal suggestions of general well-being and direct symptom disappearance, in a tone of authority and confidence. This mechanistic approach left little room for concern about the aetiology of the symptoms, although Bernheim and others, including Pierre Janet, Morton Prince, and Sigmund Freud, soon began to think in terms of multiple systems of consciousness, and to direct their attention to the underlying dynamics of the symptoms that they were treating. Freud, for example, wrote about his visit to Nancy as follows: "I witnessed the moving spectacle of old Liebeault working among the women and children of the labouring classes. I was a spectator of Bernheim's astonishing experiments upon his hospital patients; and I received the profoundest impression of the possibility that there could be powerful mental processes that nevertheless remained hidden from the consciousness of men." (Quoted by Shor, p.31, in Fromm and Shor, Hypnosis, 1972.)

An older colleague of Freud's, Josef Breuer, in the meantime, had "discovered" that the root causes of hysterical symptoms were painful memories and pent-up emotions, buried below consciousness. Pursuing this discovery, Freud and Breuer found that the hysterical symptoms could be removed by encouraging spontaneous

verbalizations by patients under hypnosis, to evoke a catharsis of
the bottled-up energies causing the symptoms. Unfortunately, Freud
soon abandoned hypnosis in favour of the free association technique
which was to become the cornerstone of psychoanalytic treatment;
and with the prominence of that method of treatment during the first
half of the last century, hypnosis again fell into disrepute – although
not into oblivion.

In one of his early books (Bright Paths to Adventure, 1945),
Gordon Sinclair told the story of Baboo Dass, a 300 pound Hindu
of average height who used to frequent the sidewalks in front of the
Imperial Bank of India on Clive Street in Calcutta. As soon as he was
seated, he would start a spiel in sing-song English telling everyone
who would listen that anything can be done by people who believe
in themselves. To prove what he meant, he would call the birds from
the air and they would gather around him. Doves, buzzards, and now
and again a parrot. These birds were called to attract attention and
to help to draw a crowd; and when sufficient people had gathered,
Baboo Dass would begin his magic tricks.

He might hand you a copper coin and tell you that if you wish
hard enough it will turn into silver, or maybe even into gold; and
Sinclair said that many people claimed the money had done just that,
although it never worked for him. But the Baboo's real secret was his
ability to give people extra strength, and for this demonstration you
had to pay a quarter or more. Then Baboo Dass would repeat his
sing-song chant about being able to do anything in the world if you'd
only … believe in yourself. Next he would pick on some little fellow
in the audience and say, "Here my friend. Lift me up. My weight is
314 pounds but you can lift me if you only believe," and some would
actually try; and much to their amazement that great hulk of a man
would come up with the ease of a baby. Sinclair, himself, tried it
several times, and I'll tell you about his experience in his own words.

"I thought at first that I must be hypnotized to the point where I
thought I was lifting the man but in truth I was not. This wasn't the
case at all. Several different visits spread over several different weeks
proved beyond doubt that I, who certainly can't lift a 200-pound

man, had easily hoisted this man of more than 300 pounds. What's more, I could hold him with ease. Even more amazing is the fact that when you are holding the old chap up he may suddenly tell you that he is about to withdraw his power from your muscles. Instantly your arms go limp and the Baboo's body slumps to the pavement. Sometimes in fact it goes down with a bruising thump. Many a scientific body has investigated Baboo Dass, indeed he is one of the prime sights of Calcutta, but none has been able to identify the hidden power he holds over the bodies of other people" (Bright Paths to Adventure, pp.166-169).

There are, of course, many other stories about people performing miraculous physical feats. There is the story of the truck driver who literally tore a car door off its hinges to free a man who was trapped in a burning car, and the mother who lifted a car off of her child that had been trapped beneath it. I tell you these stories to illustrate the fact that *there are many limitations on what we can do in our normal state of consciousness; but those same limitations may only exist for us within that normal state of consciousness*. And in other states of consciousness, those same limitations may no longer apply. In any altered state of consciousness one's normal kinaesthetic experiences may be temporarily suspended (in hypnosis, we call this dissociation), uncommon muscular rigidity may occur (catalepsy), memory may be affected (amnesia or hypermnesia), past events may be relived or revivified (age regression), a person may experience sensory input from objects which aren't there or may fail to see objects which are (positive and negative hallucinations, respectively), unusual amounts of strength may be available, and so on. *Hypnosis is about facilitating those altered states of consciousness and encouraging those unusual abilities*.

In 1938, an article appeared in the Connecticut Medical Journal, once again extolling the value of hypnosis as an anaesthetic, and this cry was soon taken up by others. Soon, the Society for Clinical and Experimental Hypnosis was founded, and by the 1960's hypnosis had been accepted by both the British and American Medical Associations both for the treatment of psychoneuroses and in hypno-anaesthesia;

and once again, the seemingly magical properties of hypnosis began to be widely recognized and accepted, not only among practitioners but by the scientific community as well. Once again, hypnosis was becoming respectable.

Five years earlier, Alfred Korzybski's magnum opus, *Science and Sanity: An Introduction to Non-Aristotelian Systems and General Semantics* (1933) noted that most Western languages are based on classical Aristotelian logic in which it is taken for granted that all judgments about what goes on in the world can be broken up into simple statements in which something (a predicate) is asserted about something else (a subject). Examples are, "water is wet" and "grass is orange." It is assumed that such statements are either "true" or "false" – "water is wet" is a true preposition; "grass is orange" is usually a false one. This is what has been called a "black and white" way of viewing the world: things are either inside of a class or outside of it. And I might mention that this form of thought was accepted without comment and taught in our schools and universities from the days of Aristotle until the mid-19th century.

Korzybski argued that "human knowledge of the world is limited both by the human nervous system and the languages humans have developed, and thus no one can have direct access to reality, given that the most we can know is that which is filtered through the brain's responses to reality." (Wikipedia). His observation that "the map is not the territory" was intended to remind us not to confuse perception (through which we create our subjective reality) with the objective reality that is being perceived.

Whatever objective reality exists, our only contact with it is through the energy that impinges on our sense organs and the way in which our brains structure that experience. The "reality" that we live in, on a day-to-day basis, is the reality that we construct in our own minds from the sights and sounds and tastes and smells and feelings that are formed in our brains from the sensory information which we receive through our visual, auditory, gustatory, olfactory and kinaesthetic senses, *plus the language that we use to structure those sensory experiences.*

The field of general semantics has not itself won a following as an effective way of treating patients with psychological or mental disorders, but it has become part of the foundation of many other cognitive treatment approaches, particularly Neuro-Linguistic Programming (NLP).

In the early 1970's, Richard Bandler, one of the co-founders of Neuro-Linguistic Programming, was a student at the University of California, Santa Cruz, when he was asked to help edit a book based on a manuscript by Fritz Perls, the founder of Gestalt Therapy. In reading the work that he was editing, he began to say to himself, "If I just model what Fritz is doing, I can do this, too." So he set up some Gestalt therapy sessions, and these Gestalt sessions attracted the attention of an associate professor of linguistics by the name of John Grinder. In 1972, he asked Grinder for help in understanding Fritz Perls' use of language. They started working together, and one of the very first things that they did was to decide that, through this particular modelling process which Richard had been using, they could take and literally recreate *anyone's* behaviour.

They were particularly interested in modelling examples of excellence, so that anyone could actually do excellently whatever it was that was being modelled. The first person that they began to study was Virginia Satir who, until her death in 1988, was considered to be the grandmother of family therapy. People would come to her and they would actually get well, as if by magic. Richard and John looked at what Virginia did, and they looked at her book, Conjoint Family Therapy, and they discovered a series of questions that she used to ask. This particular series of questions became the basis for the NLP Meta Model (that is, a model of the client's model of the world, as reflected in his or her language), which became Richard's M.A. thesis and was later published as *The Structure of Magic, Volume I* (1975). In it, they noted that "Virginia Satir and others we know seem to have this magical quality. To deny this capacity or to simply label it... genius is to limit one's own potential as a people-helper.... Our desire in this book is not to question the magical quality of our experience of these therapeutic wizards, but rather to show that this magic which they perform... has structure and is, therefore, learnable, given the appropriate resources." (Bandler and Grinder, 1975, pp. 5, 6). They also noted that it is by the questions that Virginia asked that she directed her clients to become more specific about their actual experiences, which, in NLP terms, served to bring them out of trance.

Now, Richard knew Gregory Bateson through Bateson's son, with whom he shared an interest in music. And while John and Richard were writing the second volume of The Structure of Magic, Bateson got in touch with them and told them that they should go and talk to Milton Erickson who, until his death in 1980, was considered to be the greatest medical hypnotist of this century. And what they discovered when they talked to Erickson was that he was doing just the opposite of what Satir had been doing.

They had been looking at Satir and had decided that, in order to get results in therapy, what you want to do is gain greater specificity in the client's representation of the world, so that the client restores the deletions, distortions, and generalizations that interfere with his ability to function effectively in the world. And then they discovered that Erikson was doing just the opposite. He used language patterns which were vague and ambiguous. So they had to make up another model, which they called the Milton Model. At that point they wrote the two volume set, Patterns in the Hypnotic Techniques of Milton H. Erickson, M.D. Volume 1 (1976) and, with Judith DeLozier, Patterns in the Hypnotic Techniques of Milton H. Erickson, M.D. Volume 2 (1977).

About that same time, they began to develop the notion of representational systems. Recall that way back in 1933, Alfred Korzybski has coined the phrase, "The map is not the territory," to draw attention to the mistaken belief which most of us have that our internal representations of events are identical with the events themselves. Building on that foundation, Richard and John observed that different people draw their maps with different coloured pencils, as it were. Some people have an internal representational system which is primarily auditory in nature. The internal reality in which they live is constructed primarily of words. Others are primarily visual; the building blocks which they use to construct reality are pictures. Still others are primarily kinesthetic; and they think in terms of feelings.

Now, what does all this have to do with hypnosis? The answer lies in the fact that leading your client from one representational system to another will result in an altered state of consciousness, which Bandler and Grinder claim is synonymous with hypnosis.[2] In most systems of hypnosis this is accomplished through a two stage process known as "pacing" and "leading." Pacing refers to verbalizing and otherwise acknowledging and matching the ongoing conscious experience of the client, while leading refers to gradually shifting the client toward a different way of experiencing reality. For example, if your client is using a primarily kinaesthetic representational system because, for example, she has arthritis in the fingers of one hand, you might say something like (paraphrasing Bandler and Grinder, 1981, p.19) "You can feel the pain in your hand, and it hurts, ... but you can also feel the beating of your heart, the feel of your feet within your shoes, and your glasses on your nose. You can feel the heaviness within your body as you ... let yourself relax and ... sink comfortably into your chair." You begin by making statements that are easily verified by your client, gaining credibility by matching her experience; and then, by introducing elements that are just outside her momentary awareness, you gradually lead her into an altered state of consciousness. For example, through reference to the feeling of her feet within her shoes, you provide your client with a covert instruction to change her present consciousness. But once you have established even minimal rapport, you can effect an even larger change by making statements that direct attention to other sensory modalities: "And you can hear the sound of my voice, and as you listen to my instructions, you can ... let yourself become deeper and deeper relaxed. Smooth out your forehead. Relax the muscles of your eyes. Imagine, if you like, gazing off into the distance at some calm

---

2   In 1981, Bandler and Grinder published another seminal work on hypnosis, *Trance-Formations: Neuro-Linguistic Programming and the Structure of Hypnosis* (Connirae Andreas, ed).

and pleasant scene. Perhaps you are walking along a country road, listening to the hum of the insects and the chirping of the birds, feel the soft breezes rustling through the leaves, and watch the gentle grasses blow. ... Or perhaps you have been walking along the beach, with the warm sun shining down upon you, listening to the gentle lapping of the waves. Perhaps you can ... smell the sea and taste the salt upon your lips." Continue to lead, building a full experience in imagination to replace the one your client left behind. Then, as you achieve confirmation of the altered state through feedback which you will obtain by closely monitoring your client, pace the altered state to ratify the trance. That is, the appearance of your client should change to match her new experience, and if you watch closely you should see those changes; and, as you verbalize those changes, you confirm or ratify the trance.

Lankton (1980) recommends that two additional steps be interposed between pacing and leading, and while I don't know that they are essential for hypnosis, I believe that they are helpful, so I will just mention them here. They are: dissociating parts of the client's personality and establishing a learning set. The first is accomplished through statements such as "Let your mind remain alert while your body learns to relax" ... or ... "And now I'm going to give your unconscious mind some instruction. It isn't important whether or not your conscious mind listens to it. Your unconscious mind will hear it, and it will always stay with you in your unconscious mind." The second step which Lankton mentions, establishing a learning set, can be stimulated by statements such as "Now, in learning hypnosis, it is not essential that you ... understand what you have learned. What is important is the acquisition of knowledge, and having it ready to utilize when the proper situation comes along."

Now, what is the point of all these references to the unconscious mind. Well, in point of fact, it is probably just a ploy that serves no other purpose than confusing the subject and introducing a little mystery into her life. However, it could be more meaningful than your average hypnotist will ever know, because where do you suppose the Gods really went when man became conscious those many years ago? You don't really believe that stars are the windows of heaven, where angels peek through, do you? Well, perhaps you do, but I want to offer you an alternative conceptualization.

According to Paul MacLean, a noted neuro-physiologist who served as chief of brain evolutionary research at the National Institute of Mental Health, the human brain evolved over millions of years from the brain of lower animals. But this evolution took place in three main stages, says MacLean, and thus the human brain has three main parts. MacLean calls this the theory of the triune brain. The first animals to develop a true brain were the ancient reptiles. This reptilian brain still exists inside your head, says MacLean, in the form of your brain stem. The stem of your brain sits atop your spinal cord, and reaches up to your cerebrum, much as the stem of a mushroom reaches from the roots of the plant up to the big, fleshy cap. Your brain stem includes such neural structures as the pons and the medulla, which help control such vital activities as walking, breathing, swallowing, and adjusting your heart rate. The brain stem is also the main pathway for conducting messages between your brain and your spinal cord.

Over millions of years, the ancient mammals evolved from the reptiles. And in the evolutionary process, MacLean says, many additional neural structures got tacked onto the reptilian brain. MacLean calls these 'tacked on' nerve centers the old mammalian brain. The most important parts of this old mammalian brain are the thalamus, the hypothalamus, and the limbic system. Your thalamus acts like a giant switchboard which routes sensory input to the proper areas of your brain and output commands from your brain to your muscles. It is involved in motivation, while your limbic system is responsible for such primitive emotional reactions as sex and aggression.

According to MacLean's theory, as the mammals themselves evolved (from rat to cat to elephant to monkey), they acquired the huge cerebral hemispheres that make up the major part of the human brain. MacLean calls this the new mammalian brain, which is composed of the cerebrum (including the cerebral cortex), the corpus callosum (the connecting pathway between the two cerebral hemispheres), and the cerebellum or "little brain," a large centre of neural tissue at the rear of the brain that is involved in the co-ordination of muscle movements.

Now, most people are right handed and, as you know, in right handed people, particularly in males, speech is more-or-less localized in the left cerebral hemisphere of the brain, whereas certain other functions are localized in the right cerebral hemisphere. Left hemisphere functioning tends to make use of digital information. It tends to remember and recognize names, to respond to verbal instructions, to rely on words for meaning, to produce logical thoughts and ideas, to be serious and systematic and planful in solving problems, to deal with problems sequentially, one at a time, to be critical and analytic in reading or listening and understanding, to use language in remembering, and to be receptive to abstract truths.

The right hemisphere, in contrast, tends to make use of analogical information. It is primarily responsible for recognizing and remembering faces, for responding to visual and kinaesthetic instructions, for interpreting body language easily, for responding to metaphors and analogies and emotional appeals. It is synthetic and holistic in thinking, intuitive in problem solving, creative and associative and playful. In fact, according to McConnell, "there is a striking parallel between [Freud's] descriptions of 'conscious' and 'unconscious' mental processes and the functions shown by the left and right hemispheres..." of the brain (1983, p.47); and it is the unconscious which we evoke when we engage the right hemisphere of the brain. Again, to the extent that our ordinary state of consciousness is governed by the left hemisphere of the brain, ... you will induce hypnosis as you assist your client to suspend logical reasoning and to enter a world of music, intuition, metaphor, imagination and dream.

Of course, interesting as these phenomena may be, none is important except as ... they may be used to ... enrich your life and the lives of those with whom you come in contact. Dissociation is useful, for example, to help you ... overcome unnecessary fears and ... leave those maladaptive learnings from the past behind. Memory for pleasant events can be enhanced, enabling you to ... retrieve those situations in which you have attained success, and to ... experience again the feelings which you still have ... at such times. And you know that we all ... forget many things; and it is particularly pleasant to ... forget about the unpleasant things that have happened to you in your life, so that ... you may ... move forward to the joy and comfort and achievement and satisfactions which ... you will realize in the future, and the contributions that you can make to the lives of those who need your special help.

Now, if we suppose that these new and magical abilities can frequently be found by a person who is in an altered state of consciousness as a result of moving from left hemisphere to right hemisphere functioning, how can the hypnotist facilitate such change? Well, the field of hypnosis is largely composed of techniques for accomplishing just that. In describing the hypnotic techniques of Milton Erickson, Bandler and Grinder suggest that Erickson used language in hypnosis primarily to accomplish two related tasks: distraction and ... or utilization of the dominant hemisphere (the conscious mind), and accessing the non-dominant hemisphere (the unconscious mind).

First let us consider the distraction and ... or utilization of the dominant hemisphere. Erickson suggests that, whether or not relaxation is essential for psychological treatment, it is useful because it facilitates the hypnotic subject's beginning movement away from his normal state of consciousness. That is, it gently helps the client to ... stop defending the status quo. He also uses pacing to accomplish the same objective. By verbalizing an accurate description of the client's ongoing experience, both observable and non-observable, he creates a type of "yes set." The client is willing to ... listen to him because he is able to demonstrate that he ... knows what he is talking about.

Distraction and ... or utilization of the dominant hemisphere, however, can also be accomplished somewhat more subtly and indirectly. In discussing his work with facilitating problem solving in patients, for example, Erickson (Erickson, Rossi, and Rossi, 1976) suggests that the dimming of outer reality (what he calls "depotentiating habitual frames of reference"), leading to confusion and a receptivity to clarifying suggestions, can be facilitated by introducing paradox and double binds; by using shock and surprise, the unrealistic and the unusual, all in the interest of freeing the patient from the tyranny of his usual limited frames of reference. Being Erickson, of course, he also uses depotentiation of the client's habitual frame of reference as an induction procedure in its own right, one which he calls "the confusion technique."

Just ... pay close attention to this example, which was designed to help a patient with chronic pain and ... you will know what I mean: "And just as you wish there were no pain, you know that there is, but what you don't know is ... no pain ... is something you can know. And no matter what you know, no pain would be better than what you know ... and of course what you want to know is ... no pain ... and that is what you are going to know, no pain. You wish to know no pain but comfort ... and you do know comfort ... and no pain ... and as comfort increases you know that ... you cannot say no to ease and comfort ... but you can say no pain and know no pain but know comfort and ease, and it is so good to know comfort and ease and relaxation and to know it now and later and still ... longer and longer as more and more relaxation occurs ... and wonderment and surprise come to your mind as you begin to know a freedom and a comfort you have so greatly desired ... and as you feel it grow and grow you know and really know that today, tonight, tomorrow, all next week and next month that the wonderful feelings which you have had in the past seem almost as clear as if they were today ... and the memory of every good thing is a glorious thing. And now you have forgotten something, just as we all forget many things, good and bad, especially the bad because the good are good to remember ... and you can ... remember comfort and ease and relaxation and restful sleep ... and now that you know that you need no pain and it is good to know ... no pain ... and good to remember, always to remember that in many places, here, there, everywhere you have been ... at ease and comfortable ... and now that you know this, you know that no pain is needed ... but that you do need to ... know all there is to know about ease and comfort in relaxation ... and numbness and dissociation and the redirection of thought and mental energies ... and to know and fully know all that will give you freedom to know and to enjoy unimpeded the pleasures of being comfortable and at ease, and that is what you are going to do." If you have been paying very close attention to that induction, you will notice that it tends to overload the cognitive system, with the result that the client is likely to become more receptive to clarifying suggestions.)

Visual imagery, as in the guided fantasy, is one of the commonest methods used for accessing non-dominant hemisphere functioning. "The hypnotist needs only to ... ask the client to visualize to ... begin the process of trance induction effectively." (Bandler and Grinder, 1975, p.186). Another common technique is having the client count, or counting for the client. "This technique serves several purposes. In the present context, the counting technique is a special case of visual accessing of the non-dominant hemisphere. When a client is listening to himself or someone else count, he is quite likely simultaneously to represent the numerals which he is hearing as an internal visual display. Numerals, as with other standard visual patterns, are stored in the non-dominant hemisphere: thus, the counting technique accesses the unconscious part of a client's brain. The relative ineffectiveness of counting as a trance induction and deepening technique for certain clients now becomes understandable – these are clients whose ability to access the non-dominant hemisphere for visual representations has yet to be developed. With this understanding of the counting task as a special case of visual accessing of the non-dominant hemisphere, hypnotists who are working with clients who have some ability to see visual representations in their mind's eye may increase the effectiveness of this technique simply by instructing the client, for example, that, as he sits there breathing rhythmically, listening to the sound of the voice counting, he is to make clear, focused images of each of the numerals as he hears its name, each in a different colour. Listening to the client's use of predicates for identifying the client's most highly valued representational system will allow the hypnotist to easily decide whether a visualization accessing induction will be effective." (Bandler and Grinder, 1975, p.187).

The use of melody as a technique for accessing the unconscious portion of the human mind is also specifically mentioned by Erickson: "...A musician, unresponsive to direct hypnotic suggestion, was induced to recall the experience of having his thoughts haunted by a strain of music. This led to a suggested search for other similar [memories]. Soon he became so absorbed in trying to recall forgotten melodies and beating time as a kinaesthetic aid that a deep trance... [developed]...." (Erickson, 1967, p.30, quoted in Bandler and Grinder, 1975, p.192).

It is not my intention in this paper to exhaust either you or the variety of techniques that hypnotists have used for trance induction. Rather, I have merely wanted to draw you a map which you might use to ... begin to find your way about in this most fascinating field. In the map which I have created for this magical mystery tour, a brief pathway cuts across a corner of the land of magic, just enough so that you may ... be aware that there are societies other than our own, each with its own language, and customs, and belief systems, foreign to us but possessing a certain validity within the boundaries of that foreign land. Then we come to the major arteries, which I will highlight for you (using a magic marker, of course). First, there is the field of hypnosis, the magnetic properties of which have interfered with many a compass and led many a traveller astray. But then we pass the town of Nancy and enter a purely psychological realm where concentration and suggestion become the order of the day. In our travels, we pass Vienna (where we can glance aside to see the microcosm that Freud created) and in doing so become conscious of the unconscious, and the role which it plays in everyday life.

Our next road leads to America and Korzybski's examination of the complex ways in which our language guides our thoughts and determines what we will and will not see, or hear, or feel, as the neuro-linguistic programmers were soon to point out.

In California, we learned about primary representational systems, the fact that different people draw their maps in different kinds of ways, and that ... moving from one representational system to another will result in an altered state of consciousness, which some would claim is synonymous with hypnosis. Next we travelled to the National Institute of Mental Health, and considered the parallels between left and right hemisphere functioning and the conscious and unconscious minds.

Finally, we travelled to Arizona to listen to the words of the greatest medical hypnotist of all time, Dr. Milton Erickson, and to ... learn from him some of the ways in which he depotentiates habitual frames of reference by distracting and ... or utilizing the dominant hemisphere (the conscious mind) and in which he accesses and facilitates non-dominant hemisphere functioning (the unconscious mind). Here [hear], you may (remember, you may have become somewhat confused, but you will) recall being reassured that ... it is not important that your conscious mind understands everything it hears, for ... your unconscious ... mind will know more than you will ever know, and it will keep that knowledge for you to use when the proper situation comes along.

I hope that, in this brief introduction, I have been able to point you in the proper direction and perhaps even assist you along the way. However, please remember that the map is not the territory; there are many other ways of describing the field of hypnosis. There are, after all, no truths to be found in the magician's bag of tricks – only new and different descriptions of new and different worlds in which new and different abilities can be found. I wish you well on your upcoming journey.

Now, before leaving this brief introduction to hypnosis, I want to illustrate for you some of the principles of hypnotic induction, using a simple relaxation exercise – assuming that you are not normally relaxed.. Enjoy the induction for its own sake and for what ... it can teach you about hypnosis. And if you wish, you may ... let your body relax in response to the hypnotic instructions, even as you keep your mind alert in response to your desire to learn more about the process.

Relaxation Instructions (RR #17)

The instructions which follow have been designed to help...you learn, too...relax.[3] Although these instructions do have a hypnotic quality, it is not intended that...you should be hypnotized by them; but keep your mind alert, while your body learns, too...relax.

Before we begin, would you please ensure that your clothing is loosened, so that your breathing and circulation are not obstructed; and in your mind's eye, open yourself...to the experience of relaxation.

Take a few moments to make yourself comfortable. And after you have made yourself comfortable, just close your eyes gently, and think of peace...of quiet...of tranquility...of slowing down. And as you do so, you will...notice that...your breathing is becoming slow and regular, and you are becoming more and more...relaxed. Enjoy the relaxation, the comfortable breathing, the feeling of calmness and peace, as... nervous tension gradually gives way to relaxation.

Now, take a deep breath, and let it all out. Stretch the muscles of your chest and throat, and let them...relax. And let your breathing become even more slow and regular, as you...sink even more deeply relaxed. Let the muscles of your arms...relax. Let them go. Let...both your arms sink soft and loose. And now your legs: let...all the muscles of your legs relax. The muscles of your lower legs...relax...the muscles of your upper legs and thighs.

And now, relax the muscles of your stomach...relax...the muscles of your abdomen and lower back...relax...the muscles of your chest and shoulders. Let your shoulders hang loosely; very, very peaceful and calm. Smooth out your forehead; relax...the muscles of your eyes. Remember that it requires effort even to maintain a facial expression, and let your face become vacant, and completely without expression. Nothing is important at this moment except the sound of my voice, and attaining a state of deep, pleasant... relaxation. An alert mind in a relaxed body. A state of peacefulness and calm.

---

3   When a space has been replaced by ... it indicates a tiny pause, a sort of "stutter step" in delivery, so as to emphasize whatever follows it immediately.

You may yawn, if you wish; stretch the muscles of your throat, and then...let them relax. So tired and peaceful; so sleepy. Imagine, if you wish, that...someone is coming to the door, and you want them to think that...you are sound asleep. Take a peek, if you wish, and... see them at the door, but then...close your eyes and imagine that...you are sound asleep; and drift and dream with me, while you experience the peacefulness of deep, pleasant relaxation.

As you...continue breathing deeply and comfortably and rhythmically, I would like you to...imagine that you are standing at the top of a gentle carpeted stairway. It doesn't matter whether...you can…see it clearly, or vaguely, or even not at all. You've been at the top of a stairway before, and you will be again. All that matters is for you to...know that in a moment, I am going to ask you to...begin to count backwards with me from twenty, while you go slowly down the stairs. And…notice how much more comfortable and relaxed you can feel, as you...go slowly down the stairs.

Twenty...nineteen...eighteen...seventeen...sixteen. Pause, and notice that...with each number that you count, and even with each even breath that you take, you are becoming even more deeply relaxed.

Fifteen...fourteen...thirteen...twelve...eleven. Already half-way down the stairs, and perhaps beginning to...notice that you can... easily understand these instructions, even though you may not consciously attend to what I am saying, and these instructions can stay safely tucked away in the back of your mind, available for you to...use whenever you need to become deeply relaxed again.

Ten...nine...eight. And perhaps beginning to...notice that any sounds that you hear can become part of your experience of comfort and well-being, so that nothing bothers and nothing disturbs.

Seven...six...five. And perhaps...you can experience feelings of heaviness and warmth spreading throughout your body; or perhaps... your body feels as if it is floating on soft, billowy clouds, as light as a feather, as if it could just float comfortably away; or perhaps...you may notice that you don't even have to be aware of your body at all – just the feeling of comfort and well-being, as…you become more and more deeply relaxed. I really don't know, and it really doesn't matter at all.

Four. Almost to the bottom of the stairs, to a place of safety and security, where nothing bothers and nothing disturbs.

Three. Feeling more and more the real enjoyment of deep, comfortable relaxation. Perhaps beginning to wonder what to experience when you reach the bottom of the stairs, and yet knowing already how much more ready you can feel to...become even deeper and deeper relaxed, more and more comfortable, where nothing bothers and nothing disturbs.

Two. And you can...enjoy the experience, as much as you like. Enjoy the relaxation, the comfortable breathing, the feeling of peacefulness, as you...let your body become even more deeply relaxed.

One. And you are almost there. And now, ahead of you there stands a blackboard. Beside it is a big can of paint with a big paintbrush in it. Move out from the stairway, take the brush, and paint the board red. Slap the paint on; dip the brush as often as you need; cover it completely. When it is all red, picture in the middle of it a big number 7. Take the brush again, and paint the board orange. Cover it completely, slap the paint on, get around the edges, dip the brush as often as you need. When it's all orange, picture in the middle of it a big number 6. Take the brush again and paint the board yellow. Get into the corners, around the edges, dip the brush as often as you need. When it is all yellow, picture in the middle of it a big number 5. Take the brush again and paint the board green. Slap the paint on, get in around the edges, cover it completely. When it is all green, picture in the middle of it a big number 4. Take the brush again and paint the board blue. When it's all blue, picture in the middle of it a big number 3. Take the brush again, and paint the board purple. When it is all purple, picture in the middle of it a big number 2. Take the brush again and paint the board violet. Cover if all over, slap the paint on, and when it is all violet, picture in the middle of it a big number 1.

Now, turn so that…you can see in front of you a screen of trees, bushes and shrubs. When you are ready, step through that screen of trees, bushes and shrubs and find yourself in a quiet place. This place might be any place; somewhere, perhaps, that you remember from your past, or even from your future. A place where you felt happy and absolutely safe. If you like, you could put some loved ones there, perhaps from your childhood. If you put loved ones there, take a few moments to greet them and renew fond memories. In any case, enjoy the safety and security and happiness you feel in this place. Then, when you are ready, look ahead of you, and picture a gentle slope going upward toward a small hillock or knoll. Slowly make your way up that gentle slope toward the top of that little hill. Along the way, you might notice the blue sky above you, soft white fluffy clouds in the sky, and the smell of the earth and grass. Feel the gentle warmth of the sun.

When you reach the top of the rise, look over and down a gentle slope towards the sea. And notice that, between you and the sea, there is a big rock, and sitting beside the rock there is a cup, and beyond that, a stream. As you begin to walk down the slope, take off your troubles and worries and, when you reach the rock, put them under the rock, and slide the rock over them, burying them for all time. Then, take off anything that encumbers you your shoes, coat and the like, and put them on top of the rock. Take the cup from beside the rock and, when you are ready, go past the rock and step into the stream. Feel the warmth of the sun on you, and the coolness of the stream on your feet. Look down into the water and see the clear, clean, crystal water of the stream. Listen to it bubbling over your feet. Bend down and dip some water from the stream into the cup. Take a sip of the water. The water is serenity and peace. Feel the water course down into your stomach, and transfer to your bloodstream to circulate all through your body, down your legs and arms, throughout your trunk, and into your head. Take another sip of the water. The water is serenity and peace.

When you are ready to move on, you can pour the rest of the water back into the stream from which it came. Leave the cup by the stream and walk on down toward the sea, and slowly along the beach. Imagine that it is mid-July, and it is evening. The sun has not yet begun to set, but it is getting lower on the horizon. The sun is a golden blazing yellow, the sky a brilliant blue, the sand a dazzling, glistening white in the sunlight. Feel the cold, wet, firm, hard-packed sand beneath your feet. Taste and smell the salt in the air. There is a residue of salt deposited on your lips from the air around. You can taste it if you lick your lips. Hear the beating of the waves, the rhythmic lapping to and fro, back and forth of the water against the shore. Hear the far-off cry of a distant gull as you continue to walk along the beach.

And suddenly you come upon a sand dune, a mound of pure white sand. Covering the mound are bright yellow buttercups, and deep pink moss roses. You sit down on its crest and look out to sea. The sea is like a mirror of silver reflecting the sun's rays, a mass of pure white light, and you are gazing intently into this light. As you continue to stare into the sun's reflection off the water, you begin to see darting flecks of violet intermingled with the silver. Everywhere there is silver and violet. There is a violet line along the horizon, a violet halo around the flowers. And now the sun is beginning to set. With each motion of the sun into the sea you become deeper and deeper relaxed.

The sky is turning crimson, scarlet, pink, amber, gold, orange. And as the sun sets, you are engulfed in a deep purple twilight, and as you look up into the night sky, a velvety blue haze. It is a brilliant starry night. The beating of the waves, the smell and taste of the salt, the sea, the sky; and you feel yourself carried upward and outward into space, to …become one with the universe. Find your comfort in that space, while I talk to you about something that you already know a lot about – remembering and forgetting.

And I say that it is something that you already know a lot about because you do it every waking moment of your life. You remember, and then you forget, so that you can remember something else. No one can remember everything all at once, so you…let some memories move quietly to the back of your mind. I wonder, for example, whether you will be surprised, or curious, or pleased to…discover that the things that you have learned today are just the same, things that you may remember tomorrow, or the next day, or next week, or even next month. I wonder if...you will decide to...let the memory of these things rest quietly in the back of your mind, or if...you will remember gradually, or all at once. I wonder if you may remember completely, or only partially. Perhaps...you will be surprised to...notice that this is the place for memory to surface, or it may be more comfortable for you to...remember at a different place, or at another time. I don't know when...you will remember the things that I have been telling you, or where...you will remember the things that I tell you, but you will remember: whenever you...make yourself comfortable in preparation for relaxation, it can serve as a reminder...of the instructions which I have been giving you. So whenever you...remember, however... you will remember, wherever...you will remember, if ever...you will remember, it will be just fine, and perfectly natural. Whatever I have said, has been said, and is safely tucked away in the back of your mind, available for you to...use, whenever you...again make yourself comfortable in preparation for relaxation.

And I wonder...if you will...feel surprised to...notice that you can... become so deeply relaxed in such a brief period of time. And perhaps... you will...feel curious about that surprise. Surprise, curiosity, and I wonder...if you will...feel pleased to...notice that, any day you wish, you can...remember the pleasant feelings of relaxation can come flooding back to you quickly and automatically whenever you...make yourself comfortable again...in preparation for...relaxation.

Resting as you are, you can...continue to relax in the safety and security of the knowledge that, whenever you may wish to become fully awake, you may do so simply by sitting up, taking a few deep breaths, and directing your attention back to the objects around you. In the meantime, however, you are gaining more and more control over your entire mind and body. You are becoming more and more skilled at relaxation. This skill will enable you to...think about and deal constructively with life's problems without interference from unnecessary nervous tension. Again, let me remind you that relaxation is a skill that comes with practice, and as you...continue to...follow these instructions, you will...find it more and more easy to relax, when you again make yourself comfortable in preparation for relaxation, and throughout your daily life as well.

Of course, it will always be entirely up to you, whether...you will let yourself become deeply relaxed, and if, at any time in the future, you may find if inconvenient to relax, you will stay just as tense as you may wish to be. In addition, you will recall, if at any time while deeply relaxed, you may wish to become fully awake, you may do so simply by sitting up, taking a few deep breaths, and directing your attention back to the objects around you. However, when you...do let yourself become deeply relaxed, you will find that it is a very pleasant and rewarding experience, and that, when you awake, you will... feel refreshed and rested. But rest now, rest, whether with your eyes closed or with your eyes open. That's right, you have...not left...your pleasant state of...relaxation.

In a few moments, I am going to ask you to arouse yourself, but till then, just remain resting peacefully, and really enjoy the feelings that your body can give you, so that, *in a moment*, when I count from one to five, you will be able to...feel yourself returning up the stairs, walking or floating gently, and feeling refreshed and rested and oh, so good all over. More alert with every number that I count. No need to hurry; you can have all the time that you want. After all, time is relative, and you can...feel yourself returning slowly, comfortably up the stairs; more alert with every number that I count; perhaps surprised that...you can...feel so well. Comfortable, and feeling well.

Now, bring that feeling of comfort and well-being with you as you make your way back along the beach and past the stream – retrieving any of your belonging that you left there – to the bottom of the stairs, and when you are ready, begin to slowly climb or let yourself float back up the stairs to full waking consciousness. One: Beginning to arouse yourself as you journey back up those stairs to full waking consciousness. Two: Open your eyes wide and look around you. Three: When you reach the top, take a few deep breaths and direct your attention back to the objects around you. And Four: Wake up. Wake up. Wide awake, and feeling rested, refreshed, and feeling well all over. I trust...you...enjoyed these few brief moments of relaxation.

CHAPTER 2

On Being Perfect[4]

In his ground-breaking book on psychotherapy from a communication perspective (Strategies of Psychotherapy, 1963), Jay Haley noted that all human communication attempts both to convey information and to influence or control the relationship within which that communication occurs, and that *symptomatic* behaviour communicates an attempt by the patient to control the relationship without having to accept responsibility for doing so. It is the job of the therapist, therefore, to interact with the patient in such a way that the patient is *not* able to control the relationship by behaving symptomatically, thereby not rewarding the patient for symptomatic behaviour, so that it has an opportunity to die out or "extinguish."

In *The Art of Psychoanalysis*, Haley comments that the patient begins by offering his symptoms while saying that he cannot help behaving the way he does, that he is not in control of his own behaviour. The therapist doesn't deny this, nor does he deny the patient's feeling that he ought to be in control. Instead, he accepts the patient as he presents himself, symptoms and all. But then the therapist suggests that there are unconscious reasons for the patient's difficulty, placing the locus of responsibility within the patient but not within his conscious control, and defining the task as one of making the unconscious conscious. The idea of the "unconscious" enables the patient to express and talk about himself without owning the responsibility for what he says and

---

4   A slightly edited version of a paper was presented at a Theology Colloquy held at Graceland College, Iowa in February, 1996.

does. This pattern of communication is, of course, the same as using one's symptoms to control the relationship: "It is happening, but I am not responsible for it." By assuming an unconscious, however, the therapist accepts and encourages the problematic behaviour while, at the same time, preventing the patient from using it to control him.

In due course, the bind that the patient is in becomes critical. He is constrained from getting out of it by quitting the relationship because the therapist has defined that as unconscious resistance to treatment. He cannot force the therapist to make decisions for him, because the relationship is always being defined by the therapist as supportive but nondirective. He cannot break out of the situation by aggression because the therapist simply accepts attacks by questioning their motivation. Haley suggests that, at this point, the patient can only escape from the bind that he is in by either ceasing to try to control the therapist symptomatically or by acknowledging that he is trying to do so, and the easiest solution is frequently for the patient to effect a cure.

Alan Watts (Psychotherapy: East and West, 1961), however, feels that the process is somewhat more complicated than this. In addition to the fact that the patient is trying to control the therapist through his symptomatic behaviour – unconsciously, of course – is the fact that he is trying to get help without having to become aware of himself. According to Watts, the patient is so disturbed by the discrepancy between his self-image and how he actually behaves that he dare not let himself become fully aware of it, although he wouldn't be coming for treatment at all unless he were at least dimly aware that this discrepancy is causing him some problems. In psychotherapy, therefore, the therapist (in effect) taunts the patient by suggesting that he cannot really conceal himself, while demonstrating an attitude of complete acceptance and respect. At the same time, throughout this interaction, the therapist is implicitly testing two premises which the patient has assumed to be correct. The first is that some of his actions are his own, and that they proceed freely from the choices that he makes – which the therapist challenges by asking whether behaviour that the patient believes to be voluntary is really so. The second is that some of his actions are not his own, and that they happen against his will – which the therapist challenges by attributing intent to involuntary behaviour, by suggesting, for example, that there is meaning in the patient's dreams. This places the patient in a double bind because it implies that however he behaves, either "voluntarily" or "involuntarily," he reveals himself to the therapist. Again, if he leaves the field, he is resisting. If he blocks, the therapist will gently imply that this too is revealing, and that there must be something which he is anxious to conceal from himself. And if he aggresses against the therapist, that too is revealing. With repetition, the patient eventually learns that all his attempts at self-concealment are absurd, and that his only escape is simply to be what he is without restraint. He does not simply learn to "be himself" as if that were something which one can do; he learns rather that there is nothing that he can do to not be himself.

Now, the Bible contains a number of injunctions to be perfect, but for purpose of illustration, one should suffice. From the fifth chapter of Matthew:

> [Mat 5:45] Ye have heard that it hath been said, Thou shalt love thy neighbour, and hate thine enemy.
>
> [Mat 5:46] But I say unto you, love your enemies; bless them that curse you; do good to them that hate you; and pray for them which despitefully use you and persecute you;
>
> [Mat 5:47] That ye may be the children of your Father who is in heaven; for he maketh his sun to rise on the evil and on the good, and sendeth rain on the just and on the unjust.
>
> [Mat 5:48] For if ye love only them which love you, what reward have you? Do not even the publicans the same?
>
> [Mat 5:49] And if ye salute your brethren only, what do ye more than others? Do not even the publicans the same?
>
> Mat 5:50] Ye are therefore commanded to be perfect, even as your Father who is in heaven is perfect.

And thereby lies a tale because, while the idea of being perfect "even as God is perfect" is an interesting one, this injunction to be perfect has probably done more harm than good, as J.B. Phillips (Your God Is Too Small, 1952) has observed:

> "Of all the false gods there is probably no greater nuisance in the spiritual world than the 'god of one hundred per cent'. For he is plausible. It can so easily be argued that since God is Perfection, and since He asks the complete loyalty of His creatures, then the best way of serving, pleasing, and worshipping Him is to set up absolute one-hundred-per-cent standards and see to it that we obey them. After all, did not Christ say, 'Be ye perfect'?" (p. 25)

In religious circles, however, they call this scrupulosity, and it is considered to be a false virtue, and one to be avoided as an obstacle to spirituality. For in fact, *at any given moment in time*, no one can ever be anything other than what he or she is. We may *strive* to perfect ourselves but, like life, perfection is a journey rather than a destination, properly a verb rather than a noun. Except in the sense of being *perfectly human* – and we are all good at that – perfection is an ideal rather than a reality.

> "The Hasidic tradition offers numerous stories intended to remind human beings that we are not in ultimate control, that we are not all-powerful, that we are not God." (Kurtz and Ketchum, p.21)
>
> "When the disciples of the Baal Shem Tov [Israel, son of Eliezer, the founder of the Hasidic movement in the eighteenth century] asked him how to know whether a celebrated scholar whom they proposed to visit was a true *zaddik* [i.e., a rabbi who lives an exemplary life], he answered:
>
> 'Ask him to advise you what to do to keep unholy thoughts from disturbing you in your prayers and studies. If he gives you advice, then you will know that he belongs to those who are of no account.'" (p. 16)

Furthermore, with respect to perfection, even if we wanted to be perfect, none of us knows any more than where to begin, seeing "through a glass darkly" as we surely do; and few of us even know *that*, since few of us even know where we are to start with, poor ignorant creatures that we are. The best we can do is to realize that we are not yet perfect and, like the Man of La Mancha, dream *The Impossible Dream:*

> "This is my quest, to follow that star, no matter how hopeless, no matter how far, to fight for the right without question or pause, to be willing to march into hell for a heavenly cause." (Lyrics by Joe Darion)

– or as Robert Browning (Andrea del Sarto, 1855) said:

> Ah, but a man's reach should exceed his grasp,
> Or what's a heaven for?

Of course, it isn't quite that simple. Men, in particular – as opposed to women – have a tendency to put their ideals ahead of everything else, to the detriment of people. As Robert Powell (1961) says:

> "Basically ...all ideation [i.e., the forming of ideas] is harmful because concepts hypnotize us into faulty perception and wrongful thinking. It divides the individual against himself and separates him from the rest of creation.... And of course, it does not stop at that.... the self further divides itself into good and bad, godly and devilish, conscious and unconscious, etc. – thus causing man to be at war with his own humanity. [Quoting from Hsin-hsin Ming, the oldest Zen poem, he writes]:

A split hair's difference, And heaven and earth are set apart!
(The Great Awakening, pp. 44-45)

"...when 'heaven and earth are set apart,' there is ever the struggle between what *is* and what *should be*...." (Op cit., p.46)

Furthermore,

"Where there is ideation, there is definition, where there is definition there are divisions and labels – the labels then become slogans and banners; the banners so easily become 'causes' – and then causes for war and all the other miseries such as concentration camps, brainwashing, nuclear weapons, etc." (Powell, op cit., p. 47-48).

And as they used to say in the 1960's, "War is not healthy for children and other living things." So perhaps it is fortunately that there is more to life than living up to ours or someone else's ideals,

"One day Mohammed was offering prayer at the mosque. Among the people praying with the Prophet was an Arab aspirant.

Reading the Koran, Mohammed recited the verse in which Pharaoh makes the claim, 'I am your true God.' On hearing this the aspirant was so filled with spontaneous anger that he broke the silence and shouted, 'The boastful son of a bitch!'

The Prophet said nothing, but after prayer was over the others began to scold the Arab. 'Aren't you ashamed of yourself? You have surely displeased God because not only did you interrupt the holy silence of prayer but you used filthy language in the presence of God's Prophet.'

The poor Arab trembled with fear, until Gabriel appeared to Mohammed and said, 'God sends greetings to you and wishes you to get these people to stop scolding that simple Arab; indeed, his spontaneous profanity moved my heart more than the holy prayers of the others.'" (Kurtz and Ketchum, p. 30)

Thus, even our imperfections can sometimes help to keep us in touch with God. In fact, as Lehi said to his eldest son, Jacob (Book of Mormon, 2 Nephi 1: 81-115):

> "... it must needs be that there is an opposition in all things. If not so, my first born in the wilderness, righteousness could not be brought to pass; neither wickedness; neither holiness nor misery; neither good nor bad.
>
> ...Now, behold, if Adam had not transgressed, he would not have fallen; but he would have remained in the garden of Eden. And all things which were created must have remained in the same state which they were, after they were created; and they must have remained forever, and had no end. They would have had no children; wherefore, they would have remained in a state of innocence, *having no joy, for they knew no misery; doing no good, for they knew no sin. But, behold, all things have been done in the wisdom of him who knows all things.* [italics added] Adam fell, that men might be; and men are, that they might have joy."

In 1991, Ragini Michaels published the results of a ten-year modelling project that looked into the successes and difficulties of those seeking to define their identity from a spiritual perspective. In her introductory chapter, she writes:

> "... I was eating breakfast with a friend, for probably the hundredth time, when he commented how repetitious life could be. That comment caused me to begin noticing many things – how the sun rises and sets each day – how the tide comes in and the tide goes out twice a day – how the seasons continue to shift, every year the same process, summer-fall-winter-spring – how the body requires that we eat and sleep each day. I began to realize that these seemingly unimportant repetitions were demonstrating patterns of change that could teach me something important the about how to live."

Reg M. Reynolds

She went on to remark that "The most basic pattern all of us experience is change..." and that inside of that pattern of change is woven a pattern which she called the Facticity of Opposites. Everything seems to have a dual nature, and we tend to set up what we like against what we dislike, forgetting that "spring only arises out of the winter, and the beauty of the stars can only be seen because of the night's darkness." (Facticity, pp. 2-4)

As Connirae Andreas (Core Transformation, 1994) says, when an individual embraces and cherishes any supposedly negative quality within himself, and enquires into the highest purpose which that part of himself is attempting to achieve, invariably it will be found that what is being sought is some positive state-of-being *such as* love, inner peace, or oneness with the universe or with God. Adopting that being-state as a starting point[5] rather than as a goal that is still-to-be-achieved is transformative. And having the experience of having had that way of being-in-the-world from infancy, fully integrated into oneself throughout one's life is even more freeing and transforming; and both can be had just for the asking – a gift of grace, as it were.

It is a bit like the story of Beauty and the Beast. Beauty joins the Beast only out of love for her father; but as she comes to love him as he is, he becomes loveable. His enchantment is dissolved, and he is transformed into a prince.

But hold on just a minute. Surely that only applies to those of us who are saints already! Surely it doesn't include people like any mass murderer whom you would care to name, and people like myself?

---

5   Which is not without precedent: Thomas Gordon, for example, in his book, *I'm O.K., You're O.K.*, writes that everyone, by virtue of the knowledge and power differential between adults and children, comes out of childhood feeling not O.K. about themselves. The experiences on which those feelings are based cannot be erased, but they can be set aside; and he recommends that each of us begin afresh by consciously adopting the existential position of "I'm O.K.," and that we build a whole new set of experiences based on that premise, so that any previous "I'm not O.K."-based experiences become relatively less important, and eventually insignificant, in our lives.

Oh, but it does. It includes everyone. Each of us is perfectly human and each is exactly what he or she should be *at this moment in time* (given his or her heredity and the learning experiences that he or she has had since the moment of conception). And accepting that fact of life is a good starting point for the journey towards any other goal, even one that is so far away as attaining to God's perfection.

REFERENCES

Andreas, C. and Andreas, S. (1994) *Core transformation.* Moab, Utah: Real People Press.

The Bible.

The Book of Mormon.

Haley, J. (1963) *Strategies of psychotherapy.* New York: Grune and Stratton.

Kurtz, E. and Ketcham, K. (1992) *The spirituality of imperfection.* Toronto: Bantam Books.

Michaels, R.E. (1991) *Facticity.* Seattle, Washington: Facticity Trainings.

Phillips, J.B. (1952) *Your God is too small.* London: The Epworth Press.

Powell, R. (1961, 1983) *The great awakening: Reflections on Zen and reality.* Wheaton, Ill.: The Theosophical Publishing House.

Lucinda Vardey, Ed. (1995) *God of all worlds.* Toronto: Knopf Canada.

Watts, A. (1961) *Psychotherapy east and west.* Toronto: New American Library of Canada.

CHAPTER 3

Four Kinds of Communication in Psychotherapy and Life[6]

The present paper is a review of the contributions of Robert Langs to psychotherapy, as found in books which he published during the period from 1973 to 1979. It describes an adaptational-interactional approach to psychotherapy in which attention is directed to the therapeutic and anti-therapeutic role of introjection and identification with the therapist. More specifically, Langs has been concerned with preventing iatrogenic emotional and behavioural disturbances, by teaching therapists to monitor the effectiveness of their interventions through attending to the client's commentary on them.

In writing this review, I have taken the liberty of quoting extensively from Dr. Langs' own work without, however, providing the voluminous number of quotation marks which perhaps should have been provided in order for this paper to be entirely proper. Thus, the reader should be advised that I make no claim to originality, and that my main purpose in writing this paper is to introduce to the

---

6   When I first submitted this paper to a journal for publication (as Therapeutic Interaction in the Bipersonal Field: Contributions of Robert Langs to Clinical Psychoanalysis, 1973 – 1979), probably about 1979, it was turned down because it didn't contain anything original, i.e., the reader could learn anything it has to teach just from reading these books by Langs. Now, doesn't that bizarre bit of logic boggle the mind!

broader psychological community this most brilliant analyst whose writings have not yet received the attention that I think they deserve.

In classical psychoanalysis and psychoanalytically oriented psychotherapy, the central motivating factor in the treatment situation and in the patient's communications is his intrapsychic anxieties, conflicts, fantasies, and memories. The therapist, although a participant, is essentially a passive, neutral, and flexible figure toward whom these fantasies are projected and displaced; and work is undertaken primarily around conflicts and issues outside of the therapeutic relationship. In treatment, the therapist creates the conditions for the unfolding of the patient's transference, and the emphasis is on the transference component of the relationship rather than on the interaction per se (Langs, 1978 b).

There is room in this conception for an occasional gross error on the part of the therapist, and for countertransference-based therapist input into the interaction. There is also the possibility of direct pressure exerted by the patient on the therapist to respond in some inappropriate manner, viewed in terms of unconscious efforts by the patient to repeat his past rather than to remember it. However, the major determinant of the patient's behaviour in the therapeutic interaction is conceived of as being his unconscious fantasies about the therapist or other obvious displacement figures; and the therapist's job is to receive and interpret these relationship-distorting fantasies and their underlying meaning so as to free the patient from the repetition of his past (Langs,1976 b).

It was within this classical psychoanalytic context that Langs made his first major contribution to the understanding of treatment. Beginning with the observation that the day's unfinished business is often the crucial organizer through which unconscious meanings take shape and can be recognized in the interpretation of dreams, Langs (1972) found that other types of communications from patients, such as descriptions of recent events and behaviours in and out of the treatment hour, could also be more readily understood in terms of the real-life precipitants or adaptive contexts of the major sequences of material produced by the patient in treatment. Furthermore,

Langs observed that it was frequently the therapist's behaviours, his confrontations and interpretations (and errors such as modification of the ground rules of therapy), which served as the primary adaptive context for the patient's communications during therapy. Indeed, certain types of material, such as acting out, were usually found to represent the living out of real as well as transference reactions and fantasies related to the therapist and his behaviour in the treatment situation (1976 a). Nevertheless, in his earlier writings, Langs still located many of the patient's primary adaptive tasks outside the therapeutic relationship and believed that the main job of the therapist was interpretation of the transference.

Langs (1973) next added to his model of treatment the concept of the therapeutic context. Whereas the primary adaptive task was seen as a first-level organizer of the patient's material, the therapeutic context, i.e., those indicators of difficulties and resistances within the patient which tend to call for interventions from the therapist, was seen as a second-level organizer of the patient's material. Thus, the communications from the patient were first to be understood in terms of their adaptive context, and frequently in terms of the reality of the interaction between the patient and therapist, and only then in terms of the patient's internal psychopathology. This two-level approach to transference was intended to emphasize that many intrapsychically significant reactions within the patient occur in response to the therapist's behaviours and interventions. And it was noted that these therapist behaviours could be either positive or negative, constructive or destructive, necessarily or unnecessarily hurtful, and within the framework of valid interventions or based on technical errors on the part of the therapist.

It was within the context of this two-level approach to transference that Langs (1974) then began to explore the much neglected introjective side of the patient's relationship with the therapist, and to emphasize and investigate the unconscious communications contained in the therapist's interactions with his patient. Reconceptualizing the patient's relationship with the therapist in adaptational-interactional terms, Langs noted that many of the regressions and symptoms within the patient are therapist evoked, i.e., primarily introjective in nature and based on the therapist's errors in intervening, either interpretatively or in terms of his management of the framework within which the treatment occurs. Consideration of the latter led to an increasing emphasis on maintaining a secure therapeutic "hold" on the patient through rigorous adherence to the basic ground rules of therapy, i.e., an explicit verbal agreement between the therapist and patient regarding fees, appointment times, and length of sessions; an understanding that the patient will say everything that comes to mind in his therapy sessions, without exception, and that the therapist will give the patient his undivided attention, attempt to understand the patient through what he says, and offer that understanding to the patient primarily through his interpretations of material supplied by the patient; and an understanding that the therapist will offer no other gratification to the patient. That is, there will be no physical or social contact, verbal interaction will be confined to the therapist's office during regularly scheduled appointments, the therapist will remain relatively anonymous, and confidentiality will be de rigueur.

By making use of this increased understanding of the adaptive context as an organizer of the client's communications, it became increasingly clear that much of what the patient said about outside relationships and experiences had a significant although unconscious and disguised bearing on the therapeutic interaction (Langs, 1976 a).In previous psychoanalytic writings, it had been suggested that once it is determined that the material from the patient unconsciously alludes to the therapist, it is essential for the therapist to make the added assessment of the extent to which the material also contains veridical perceptions as opposed to fantasy-based distortions, using the therapist's self-knowledge as well as clues provided in the associations from the patient. This latter resource, however, had been relatively neglected up to that point, and it is to Langs' credit that he not only recognized its significance but elaborated on its significance in treatment. The recognition that the patient unconsciously perceives the therapist's errors and, further, unconsciously attempts to call them to the therapist's attention, and

even to correct him wherever possible, proved to be the beginning
of an extensive investigation of the patient's positive and negative
responses to erroneous interventions, and of what ultimately proved
to be the patient's unconscious curative efforts on behalf of both the
therapist and himself under these circumstances (Langs, 1979 a).

This understanding of the function of the client's communications
as a commentary on the therapist's communications, albeit in symbolic
and derivative terms led to an image of the patient as an individual with
enormous unconscious, valid, and creative sensitivities rather than as
someone who is virtually always sick, distorting, misunderstanding,
and responding inappropriately, even though his perceptions of and
reactions to the therapist's behaviours may take place entirely at the
unconscious level, e.g., through references to having himself behaved
badly or done something wrong or having known someone else who
did. And this conceptualization of the therapeutic interaction as
involving the therapist's responses to interaction as involving the
therapist's responses to the patient and the patient's responses to the
therapist's responses has more recently been elaborated in terms of
a spiralling interaction within the therapeutic field (Langs, 1978 a).

Working from the idea that the patient's communications are
frequently a commentary on the therapist's interventions, Langs (1978
b) went on to describe various communicative styles among patients,
in which the reporting of analyzable derivatives (by which was meant
that, in a given session or over several sessions, the patient would
unconsciously communicate with the therapist about the adaptive
context, through meaningful indirect communications related to that
context) was but one of several options available to the patient in how
he would choose to communicate with the therapist, albeit the most
useful from the standpoint of psychoanalysis or psychoanalytically
oriented psychotherapy since this style of communication allowed
the therapist to readily interpret to the patient the unconscious
meaning of his communications. There were, in addition, at least two
communicative styles among patients which were felt to be less useful
for therapy. Some patients would report material seemingly rich in
symbolic derivatives of their unconscious fantasies but without any

apparent adaptive context to provide it with definitive meaning; and some would report a series of seemingly crucial adaptive contexts but without the accompanying meaning-laden derivative associations. Initial observations suggested that these latter styles were based on factors within both the patient and the therapist, and therefore within the therapeutic interaction.

As Langs' ideas about therapy continued to develop, so did his concern about iatrogenic illness, the symptomatology within the patient that results from psychopathology shared by both the patient and therapist. Symptom resolution was seen as resulting from (1) cognitive insights derived from the therapist's interpretations, (2) the therapist's serving as a model of integrity and "straight" communication through his adherence to sound principles of technique and maintenance of the ground rules and boundaries of the therapeutic interaction, and (3) the inevitable positive identifications with the therapist which are derived from the two former types of experience. And where previous writers had viewed the ground rules as a kind of unobtrusive backdrop for the therapeutic experience and as a means of safeguarding the transference, Langs (1976 a) emphasized more and more the importance of maintaining a firm therapeutic hold in order to allow the patient to communicate with the therapist regarding his own psychopathology rather than the therapist's.

As Langs moved further and further away from viewing psychotherapy as dealing solely with the patient's intrapsychic contents, and towards a greater emphasis on the mutual interactional aspect of the therapeutic encounter, he found himself somewhat at a loss for a vocabulary with which to communicate his growing understanding of the therapeutic process. The necessary terminology was found in the Kleinian literature. Explication of the unconscious communicative interaction between patient and therapist was particularly helped by adoption of the term projective identification (Baranger and Baranger, 1966).

Now, transference has been defined as the patient's conscious and unconscious relations with the therapist based on all prior and current object relations (i.e., relationships with others), both internal and external, beginning with the primary relationship with the breast-mother that has subsequently been internalized. In this context, projective identification is defined as an early primitive mental mechanism through which the infant splits off from consciousness painful negative internal self-representations, and omnipotently places them into the "object," usually the mother. It is a mental mechanism which matures with later development; although its earliest expressions occur before self-object differentiation is complete, its later forms occur within the context of clear object relatedness and constitute interactional efforts to place parts of one's inner self into others, so as to manage intrapsychic disturbances in interactions with others. Thus, while projection is essentially an intrapsychic defense mechanism in which parts of the inner self are attributed to others without direct interactional pressures towards them, projective identification constitutes an actual interactional effort to evoke in others some aspects of one's own inner self. Introjective identification is the complementary process through which an individual incorporates into his own self-representation and inner world the projective identifications of another. In this context, Bion(1977) speaks of the relationship between the container and the contained. This metaphor alludes to the contents which are projectively identified as being the contained, while describing the object who incorporates these contents as the container. In therapeutic interaction, one important function of the therapist is to contain the patient's pathological projective identifications, accepting them *consciously* into himself and "metabolizing" them into understandings which can be interpreted to the patient.

Langs (1978 c) then distinguished between three major communicative styles in patients and therapists. The first communicative style, which he termed Type A style, is characteristic of patients who communicate an adaptive context and analyzable derivatives of it, and who use symbolic communications to do so. The second communicative style, Type B, is characterized by projective identification and the acting out of internal conflicts, so that the patient's verbal associations usually do not yield meaningful interpretative insights into the dynamics of his behaviour. In the Type C communicative style, the adaptive context is either repressed or obliterated in the presence of seemingly rich associations, or the patient communicates entirely about either realities or trivia, or if there are significant adaptive contexts then they are not accompanied by meaningfully related indirect associations. The resistances of these patients are neither readily analyzable nor expressed in derivative form. Instead, their associations are flat and empty, or rich but without organizing meaning. They serve as an impenetrable barrier whose function is to destroy meaning rather than to convey it. The Type C communicative style is a field designed for lies and falsification, and for destruction of any real person to person interaction between patient and therapist.

In the Type A communicative field, the patient uses language to communicate with the therapist symbolically about his unconscious conflicts, fantasies, memories, introjects, and perceptions. The therapist in turn interprets the patient's verbal offerings, associations, and behaviours. In general, there is a sequential alteration between periods of resistance and revelation, with interpretive resolution of the inevitable resistances and insight into their unconscious sources and meanings, as well as insight into the patient's core fantasies and memories and the like.

In the Type B field, which is established largely through the patient's use of projective identification and the discharge of tensions through acting out, the therapist's main task is to experience and contain the patient's interactional pressures and to translate them into cognitive understanding. The main interpretation offered to the patient will be the therapist's understanding of the implications of the patient's attempts to invoke in him various roles and images. Often the therapist is under considerable pressure to intervene with these patients, and he may even have to do so in times of crisis, but he must work to develop the capacity to silently tolerate any interactional pressures until they can be cognitively understood and interpreted to the patient.

In the Type C field, the patient uses communication primarily as a barrier, for the destruction of meaning, and the destruction of relatedness. The therapist must recognize that the patient's ofttimes elaborate communications actually serve to keep the therapist from getting to know and understand him (as will be recognized when the therapist tries to organize the patient's communications around some specific adaptive context); and he must refrain from responding to the manifest contents of the material, which would only serve to maintain distance and to perpetuate and support the patient's resistance to meaningful communication. Instead, he should strive to identify those metaphorical representations of the patient's communicative style which do appear, for example, in allusions to safes, walls, dead-ends, voids, deception, and so on. Whenever possible, these metaphors should be linked to an adaptive context and their defensive-barrier function either stated or implied. Only then is derivative material, usually quite chaotic and regressive, likely to become momentarily available for interpretation.

Type A communication can only exist with any consistency within the context of a secure framework, i.e., proper management of the ground rules of therapy by the therapist. Alterations in the framework are, as a rule, a function of and tend to further evoke the Type B and Type C communicative modes. Thus maintenance of the framework of therapy is essential to the development and maintenance of a Type A communicative style which, in turn, is essential to the development of a complete understanding by the therapist of the unconscious meanings of the communications of the patient (as they relate to the patient's psychopathology, to the patient's significant genetic past, and to the actual inputs from the therapist) so that these unconscious meanings can be communicated to the patient and the resultant insights used by him in the management of his life.

Implicit in this formulation is the belief that the client cannot discuss his unconscious ideas and fantasies with the therapist directly, but can only do so indirectly, and that it is through the interpretation of this derivative communication (i.e., understanding of this derivative or symbolic communication, offered by the therapist) that these unconscious ideas and fantasies can be understood. Thus, any response to the manifest content of the client's communications, including interpretation of it in terms of past or present interactions with others, while quite possibly justified in some contexts, does not constitute treatment of the neurotic problem for which the client has sought psychoanalytically oriented psychotherapy, i.e., the bringing into consciousness of the unconscious beliefs and motivations which have led him into ineffectual living and symptomatic distress.

In this model of psychotherapy, which I believe far surpasses anything else written on the subject, it is the patient who determines the direction and extent of his communications within any given session, establishing his priorities as he shares with the therapist the various thoughts which come into his mind. The therapist, in turn, is to approach each session without desire, memory, or understanding (Langs, 1978 a) so that the interpretations which he offers to the patient may be prompted entirely by the material which the patient presents and thus be as free from bias and distortion as possible.

Since the most significant unconscious communications are most likely to derive from the therapeutic interaction itself, interventions are usually most effective when it is clear to the therapist how the patient's communications relate to the ongoing therapeutic relationship, in terms of the patient's allusions to the therapist's previous interventions and management of the ground rules of psychotherapy, a specific adaptive context, and the patient's intrapsychic anxieties, conflicts, fantasies, and memories as these relate to his interactions with significant figures in his past. Each of the therapist's interventions, in turn, will become a portion of the adaptive context for any succeeding communications from the patient, and the therapist must listen to these succeeding communications in order to determine the validity of his intervention for that patient at that time.

Langs (1978 b) discusses six basic interventions. These include silence (the preferred intervention in the absence of understanding the patient's material); establishing and maintaining the framework within which psychotherapy occurs, and rectifying and analyzing any errors in application of the ground rules of psychotherapy; playing back to the patient selected elements from among his communications in an effort to foster expression of the necessary missing communicative elements which might serve to identify an adaptive context for the patient's communications; the metabolizing and interpretation of projective identifications or attempts by the patient to evoke in the therapist behaviour which is more appropriate to some other, non-therapeutic role; and the identification of metaphors used by patients who employ the Type C communicative mode. Of these six, interpretation is the preferred mode of response.

In the course of empathically listening to the patient's material and formulating an understanding of its meaning, the therapist generates silent hypotheses and makes silent predictions which he then silently validates from the patient's continued associations before choosing to intervene. These interpretations should consider not only, or even primarily, the manifest content of the patient's communication or even those inferences which can be drawn directly from the patient's material. Although the patient's communications always have a certain manifest content from which inferences may be drawn, interventions offered to the patient on that basis tend to be isolated and intellectualized without any central dynamic meaning, and tend to be responded to by the patient in a manner which does not constitute validation of the interpretation. Such formulations can be distinguished from inferences made from the manifest content of the patient's communications organized around a specific adaptive context; and valid interpretations which begin with a specific adaptive context and organize the patient's manifest associations as derivative communications related to that adaptive context tend to be validated through the patient's subsequent communications.

To reiterate, Langs is quite emphatic in stating that the therapist should always listen to the patient for symbolic or derivative references to an adaptive context, which is not infrequently the therapeutic interaction itself. He should attend to references to the framework before all other material, to medium of expression and communicative style before content, to reality before fantasy, and to analyst before patient. He should interpret resistance before content, and interactional resistance before intrapsychic resistance. He should try to avoid asking questions and providing clarifications of his ideas since these types of interventions have usually been found to occur at points in the treatment session where the patient is working over, through displaced and disguised derivatives, some aspects of his relationship with the therapist, and usually some countertransference-based input (and typically, the therapist intervenes with a question or clarification directed towards some outside relationship or an aspect of the manifest content, and the intervention serves the purpose of offering the patient a Type B or Type C barrier to more meaningful communication).He should accept the supervision or direction offered by the patient's (oblique) references to his errors and correct them wherever possible, so that the therapy can progress (Langs, 1979 b).

There is a fourth type of communication that was not discussed by Langs, and that has been called "straight talk." This fourth kind of communication doesn't require any interpretation, and people who indulge in it are unlikely to require the assistance of a psychotherapist.

References

Bion, W. *Seven servants*. New York: Jason Aronson, 1977.

Langs, R. A psychoanalytic study of material from patients in psychotherapy. In R. Langs, *Technique in transition*. New York: Jason Aronson, 1978 b. (A version of this paper was first published in the International Journal of Psychoanalytic Psychotherapy, 1972 Vol. 1, No. 1, pp. 4-45.)

Langs, R. *The technique of psychoanalytic psychotherapy* (Vol. I). New York: Jason Aronson, 1973.

Langs, R. *The technique of psychoanalytic psychotherapy* (Vol. II). New York: Jason Aronson, 1974.

Langs, R. *The bipersonal field*. New York: Jason Aronson, 1976 a.

Langs, R. *The therapeutic interaction* (2 Vols.). New York: Jason Aronson, 1976 b.

Langs, R. *The listening process*. New York: Jason Aronson, 1978 a.

Langs, R. *Technique in transition.* New York: Jason Aronson, 1978 b.

Langs, R. Some communicative properties of the bipersonal field. In R. Langs, *Technique in transition.* New York: Jason Aronson, 1978 b. (Reprinted from International Journal of Psychoanalytic Psychotherapy, 1978 c, Vol. 7, pp. 89-161.)

Langs, R. *The supervisory experience.* New York: Jason Aronson, 1979 a.

Langs, R. *The therapeutic environment.* New York: Jason Aronson, 1979 b.

CHAPTER 4

TAGteach (Using Clicker Training with Humans)

Applied Behaviour Analysis is not without its critics. The most common complaint – not the most valid; just the most common – is that it is mechanical and dehumanizing. Unfortunately, ABA <u>can</u> be delivered in just that way, but that is extremely rare. Like any good teaching, it is a very human enterprise. Of course humans are prone to error! But the point that I want to make here is that ABA does not have to be mechanical and dehumanizing, and rarely is.

Which brings us to clicker training, which most people associate with dog training and, therefore, feel is not appropriate for use with humans. In fact, clicker training – TAGteach (Teaching with Acoustical Guidance) – has been applied very successfully in all kinds of human endeavours, from teaching surgical skills and workplace safety to training athletes and musicians. It is also being applied to teaching children with autism.

When it comes to teaching children with autism, I feel that TAGteach is so important that it is next to criminal to avoid incorporation this relatively-new-to-autism technology into your teaching! Relatively new? I was surprised to learn that Kerry Madden and Robert Hanson of Applied Behavior Consultants Inc. had written about "The Use of TAG for Children with Autism" a good ten years ago. Personally, I have been advocating for greater use of TAGteach for the past four years, without much success. However,

I have recently completed a Primary Level TAGteach certification workshop and am ready to try again.

TAGteach has been endorsed by many well known and influential ABA practitioners. Perhaps the biggest names, to get your attention, are Julie Vargas (B.F. Skinner's daughter), Mary Barbara (co-author of *The Verbal Behavior Approach: How to Teach Children with Autism and Related Disorders*), Raymond Miltenberger (former President of the Association for Behavior Analysis International and author of *Behavior Modification: Principles and Procedures*), John Eshleman (known for his work in fluency training), Rick Kubina (co-author of *The Precision Teaching Book*), and our own local Elizabeth Benedetto-Nasho (The Step by Step Learning Group) and Kevin Cauley (Adventure Place), to name just .a few.

Operant conditioning research has shown that behaviour tends to be under the control of its consequences. Some consequences – typically consequences that the learner experiences as desirable – strengthen or "reinforce" the behaviour that they follow, i.e., they make it more likely that the behaviour will occur under the same circumstances. Other consequences – typically consequences that are experienced as undesirable – tend to "punish" the behaviour that they follow, in the sense that they make it less likely that the behaviour will occur under the same circumstances.

Now, reinforcement that is provided within about ½ second after a behaviour that you wish to strengthen is more effective than reinforcement that is delayed. There are a number of reasons for that, including (1) the longer the interval between behavior and reinforcer, the harder it is for the learner to associate the behaviour with its reinforcer and (2) the greater the likelihood that some other behavior will have occurred in the meantime, and that is what will be reinforced.

Unfortunately, although the behavior that you want to teach is most effectively learned if the reinforcer can be delivered immediately, the universe is not always that accommodating. Sometimes, in spite of your best intentions, delivery of the reinforcer is going to be delayed, and the learner is actually doing something else when the reinforcer arrives. TAGteach can help to bridge the gap between the behaviour that you want your learner to learn and the reinforcer that will be provided – in effect, providing a signal that reinforcement, although delayed, will be coming.

TAGteach has many advantages:

1. Feedback is precise.
2. Feedback is always positive.
3. Having to think of successive TAG points helps to define the teaching targets.
4. TAGteach doesn't invite a social response
5. The TAG eliminates the emotion from the feedback.
6. The TAG's are easily perceived and counted.
7. There is no condescension involved
8. The trainer gets to shut up.

If you "google" TAGteach, you will find websites for TAGteach International (www.tagteach.com) and a couple of blogs (tagteachblog.com and tagteach.blogspot.com), where you will find a lot of information about TAGteach and about its use with individuals with autism (I particularly like the videos that Martha Gabler has posted). The many illustrations of its effectiveness on the TAGteach International website will, or at least should, blow you away. **There is also quite a bit of information about TAGteach and Autism on Mary's blog** (http://verbalbehaviorapproach.blogspot.ca/2010/05/tagteach-and-autism.html)**.**

I am just a beginner at using TAGteach, but I am convinced that it will be an important addition to your ABA repertoire. As I implied in the beginning, instructor therapists make a lot of errors in their teaching. Learning about and using this TAGteach methodology will help to eliminate many of them.

CHAPTER 5

How Shall We View God?

In the third chapter of Exodus, we read:

[Exo 3:1] Now Moses kept the flock of Jethro his father in law, the priest of Midian: and he led the flock to the backside of the desert, and came to the mountain of God, even to Horeb.

[Exo 3:2] And the angel of the Lord appeared unto him in a flame of fire out of the midst of a bush: and he looked, and, behold, the bush burned with fire, and the bush was not consumed.

[Exo 3:3] And Moses said, I will now turn aside, and see this great sight, why the bush is not burnt.

[Exo 3:4] And when the Lord saw that he turned aside to see, God called unto him out of the midst of the bush, and said, Moses, Moses. And he said, Here am I.

[Exo 3:5] And he said, Draw not nigh hither: put off thy shoes from off thy feet, for the place whereon thou standest is holy ground.

[Exo 3:6] Moreover he said, I am the God of thy father, the God of Abraham, the God of Isaac, and the God of Jacob. And Moses hid his face; for he was afraid to look upon God.

And a few verses later, we read:

[Ex0 3:13] And Moses said unto God, Behold, when I come unto the children of Israel, and say unto them, The God of your fathers hath sent me unto you; and they shall say to me, What is his name? what shall I say unto them?

[Exo 3: 14] And God said unto Moses, I AM THAT I AM: and he said, Thus shalt thou say unto the children of Israel, I AM hath sent me unto you.

John Spong credits one of his former seminary students, Kathrin "Katie" Ford, with the observation that "God is not a person. God is not a being. God is Being itself. ... Being itself, is not the father of life. This God *is* life." Resonating with those statements, he has added that "...we human beings cannot *know* God; we can only *experience* God."

Gregg Braden, the author of The Divine Matrix (2007), identifies this state of being as the holographic quantum universe, in which the entire universe is contained within each tiny segment of it or, as the Buddhists would have it, "The universe in a grain of sand."

In her introduction to A History of God: The 4,000 Year Quest of Judaism, Christianity and Islam, Karen Armstrong observes that:

> ...human beings are spiritual animals. ... Men and women started to worship gods as soon as they became recognizably human; they created religions at the same time as they created works of art. This was not simply because they wanted to propitiate powerful forces; these early faiths expressed the wonder and mystery that seemed always to have been an essential component of the human experience of this beautiful yet terrifying world. Like art, religion has been an attempt to find meaning and value in life, despite the suffering that flesh is heir to.
>
> ... Throughout history, men and women have experienced a dimension of the spirit that seems to transcend the mundane world. ... However we choose to interpret it, this human experience of transcendence has been a fact of life. Not everybody would regard it as divine: Buddhists, as we shall see, would deny that their visions and insights are derived from a supernatural source; they see them as natural to humanity. All major religions, however, would agree that it is impossible to describe this transcendence

in normal conceptual language. Monotheists have called this transcendence "God," ....

In Christian theology, God is the eternal Creator, the source of love, life, and truth. All things exist and have their being in God. "In the beginning God created the heavens and the earth."

Christians believe that God chooses to reveal Himself to humankind – and by the way, we refer to God as "Him" rather than as "Her" for a variety of reasons, not least of which are because Judaism, Christianity and Islam are all patriarchal societies, and because Jesus spoke of God as a loving Father.

Throughout the ages, humankind has sought to understand this God who reveals Himself to us, and has drawn up lists of His attributes. The Encyclopedia of Religion (Littlefield, Adams & Co., 1959) gives them as follows: "The prophetic Christian *conception* [italics added] of God ...represents God as a unitary, personal Being, as immutable [i.e., unchangeable], as omnipotent, as omnipresent, as omniscient, as eternal, as the Creator and Preserver of the world, as a morally perfect Being, as a righteous and loving Father."

It is probably safe to say that we don't entirely know what it means when we say that God is omnipresent. As the Apostle Paul said in his letter to the saints at Corinth, we "see through a glass darkly." God is not revealed to us in His entirety but is at least partly a mystery (to me anyway and, I suspect, to others as well).

Nevertheless, some people (such as Jacob, who felt that he had wrestled with Him) have experienced God as if God were a person, some in visions and some, such as Moses, more-or-less face-to-face. In the 12th chapter of Numbers, for example, we read: "If there is a prophet among you, I, the Lord, make Myself known to him in a vision; I speak to him in a dream. Not so with My servant Moses; He is faithful in all My house. I speak with him face to face." On the other hand, Moses himself never actually claimed to have seen God, only His back or, perhaps, where He had been.

Some hermits, in withdrawing from the world, claimed to have experienced God residing within their inmost souls. As the Muslim

mystic, Rumi, put it: "A seeker knocked at the door of the beloved –
God – and a voice from inside asked: 'Who is it?' The seeker answered,
'It is I'; and the voice said: 'In this house there is no I and You.' The
door remained locked. Then the seeker went into solitude, fasted and
prayed. A year later here turned and knocked at the door. Again the
voice asked: 'Who is it?' Now the believer answered: 'It is You.' Then
the door opened."

Others have found God in nature (as illustrated by the poem,
Vestigia, by Bliss Carman):

> I took a day to search for God
> And found Him not. But as I trod
> By rocky ledge, through woods untamed,
> Just where one scarlet lily flamed,
> I saw His footprint in the sod.

The poem continues with the sound of a bird, the feel of the wind,
the glory of the sunset, and it concludes with

> Back to the world with quickening start
> I looked and longed for any part
> In making saving beauty be....
> And from that kindling ecstasy,
> I knew God dwelt within my heart.

Then there is Brother Lawrence of the Resurrection (a 16th
Century monk who was responsible for the little tract "The
Practice of the Presence of God") who tried to live his life as if
he were actually in the presence of God – except that "as if he
were" doesn't entirely capture it because, if we believe that God
is omnipresent, he was in fact in the presence of God, as we all
are every minute of our existence -- which, of course, was entirely
in keeping with "In the ancient Jewish worldview, God is not
somewhere else. God is right here. It is God's world and God

made it and God owns it and God is present everywhere in it."
(Velvet Elvis, p. 77). He is the "Master of the Universe."

Pennington, the author of Centering Prayer – prayer in which the
petitioner listens rather than talks – knowing that God is everywhere,
writes, "We simply seek to be wholly present in love to God present
to us...." (p.74). He might as easily have written, "We simply seek to
be wholly present to the God of love present in us." Namaste!

Buddhists tend not to teach of a personal God, they do recognize
that there is a love that permeates the universe – see, for example,
Kapleau's *The Three Pillars of Zen* – and you remember, of course, that
it has been said that God is love. In the fourth chapter of 1 John, for
example, we read:

> [1 John 4:7] Beloved, let us love one another: for love is of
> God; and every one that loveth is born of God, and knoweth God.
> [1 John 4:8] He that loveth not knoweth not God; for God
> is love.

Perhaps the Christian concept of "God" is best thought of as a
metaphor for that loving spirit which permeates the universe.

Unlike other major religions, Hinduism has no historical founder,
and it has many holy books, not just one. The earliest of these scriptures
date from some time after 1500 B.C., although they weren't written
down until about 500 B.C. These include four Vedas, or collections
of hymns. The gods were invoked by singing hymns inviting them
to attend the sacrifices, and they were assumed to be present during
them. There are 33 principle deities praised in the Vedas. However,
although the hymns of the Vedas praise all of these different deities,
the Vedic sages had already formed the idea that the various deities
were all aspects of One Supreme Power, which they called "Truth."

The next set of Hindu scriptures to be developed were the
Upanishads. Important because of their philosophical teachings,
they have survived in their present form since about 200 B.C.E. They
contain the idea that there is a one-ness of all things throughout the

created universe, that the individual soul (atman) and the universal soul (Brahman), the "One God" of Hinduism, are the same; that the visible world is an illusion (maya) but that the universal soul, Brahman, is eternal, limitless, omnipresent and may be male or female. Brahman is without form, but Hindus are free to imagine this Supreme Spirit in any way that is meaningful to them, and they have done so in terms of its various aspects. Brahma (who created and continues to create the world), Vishnu (who looks after the world), and Shiva (who continually destroys part of the world so that Brahma can continue his work of creation).

Prominent among the Upanishads is the great Hindu epic, the Mahabharata, which contains many stories with a moral message. The central story of the Mahabharata is a story of the battle between good and evil, as represented by a war between the Kuru princes and their cousins, the five sons of King Pandu, over right of succession to the throne. The Bhagavad-Gita (or Song of the Lord) is a philosophical text which occurs in the sixth book of the Mahabharata. It tells the story of Arjuna, the third son of King Pandu, and his brother-in-law, Krishna, who was the king of a neighbouring country but who had volunteered to act as Arjuna's charioteer during the great war. On the eve of battle, Arjuna, seeing his kinsman ready to fight him, is filled with remorse at the thought of killing his relatives to gain a kingdom, and he turns to his charioteer for advice. It is Lord Krishna's advice concerning moral and religious values and man's relation to God that forms the text of the Bhagavad-Gita.

At one point in their dialogue, Arjuna comes to realize that Lord Krishna is actually an avatar of Vishnu, and he asks him how he would like to be worshipped. Lord Krishna replied that he actually prefers that we relate to Him as a person rather than as a disembodied spirit, since it is more compatible with human nature to do so.

But that was written a long time age and, personally, I am finding it easier to relate to God as the loving spirit that permeates the universe than to that "old man with a beard" who we were told about in our childhood, a deity modeled on mankind.

In *The Miracle of Mindfulness: A Manual on Meditation*, the Vietnamese Zen Master, Thich Nhat Hanh, tells a story about his close friend, Jim Forest. He writes: "Last winter, Jim came to visit. I usually wash the dishes after we are finished the evening meal, before sitting down and drinking tea with everyone else. One night, Jim asked if he might do the dishes. I said, 'Go ahead, but if you wash the dishes you must know the way to wash them." Jim replied, 'Come on, you think that I don't know how to wash the dishes?' I answered, 'There are two ways to wash the dishes. The first is to wash the dishes in order to have clean dishes and the second is to wash the dishes in order to wash the dishes.' Jim was delighted and said, 'I choose the second way – to wash the dishes to wash the dishes.' From then on, Jim knew how to wash the dishes. I transferred the 'responsibility' to him far an entire week."

The point of the story is to illustrate the possibility of being in the present moment, of being fully absorbed in the miracle of life, even while engaged in the most mundane of tasks – aware, appreciative, and grateful for what is.

If God is indeed omnipresent, He is not so much in need of worship as our minute-by-minute awareness of, and appreciation and gratitude for, what is – the great I AM.

> O Lord, my God, when I in awesome wonder
> Consider all the worlds Thy Hands have made
> I see the stars, I hear the rolling thunder
> Thy power throughout the universe displayed
>
> Then sings my soul, my Saviour God, to Thee
> How great Thou art, how great Thou art
> Then sings my soul, my Saviour God, to Thee
> How great Thou art, how great Thou art

CHAPTER 6

The Use of the MMPI in Teaching Personality Assessment[7]

Before beginning to talk about the use of the MMPI in teaching personality assessment, I want to say a few words about the context in which this paper was written. I am a clinical psychologist, and I work in a prison. Furthermore, in the eyes of many of my colleagues, I am an MMPI fanatic. That is, I use the test, regularly, and have done so for many years; and over the years I have come to believe that this antiquated personality test is the best instrument available for introducing students to the art, and science, of personality appraisal.

The MMPI is a curious test. It is an old test, having been put together more than 35 years ago. For a personality inventory, it is perhaps unique in having so little to say about personality traits per se. In fact, it was originally called the "Medical and Psychiatric Inventory", and it was designed to assist in the classification of medical and psychiatric patients to the Kraepelinian psychiatric nosological system in vogue at that time. Its validity rests, however, not on that diagnostic system, or on theoretical constructs, or on personality theory, but on the accumulation of empirical correlates of scales score elevations. That is, because this test has been in wide-spread use for a long time, a certain amount of actuarial data has been accumulated

_____

7   This paper was presented at a Canadian Psychological Association convention sometime around 1980. Dr. Stephen Birnstein was co-author, and he has given his permission to include this paper along with other Miscellaneous Musings.

regarding the probability of occurrence of particular kinds of behavior among groups with particular kinds of profiles, prognosis for response to different types of treatment, relative frequency of suicidal attempts, and so on – problems which are of some interest to psychologists working with particularly disturbed populations.

The MMPI is a long test. "At 566 items, it is perhaps the longest inventory on the market" (Gynther, 1972). It is very psychopathology oriented; it does not provide a well-balanced coverage of the entire domain of personality. Nevertheless, it does cover quite a wide territory. It provides a measure of the extent to which the individual differs from the average in three significant affects (anxiety, depression, and anger), in concern about mental and physical health, and in distrust of others. It provides one of the better measures of ego strength. It provides a measure of the extent to which the individual exerts intellectual control over his impulses, whether he is over-controlled or under-controlled with respect to impulse expression. It provides good measures of dominance and dependency. It provides information about the individual's relationship with his family, whether he feels that he is being hard done by, whether he is rebellious against authority, whether he is shy or outgoing, whether his affective relationships with others are impaired, whether he is isolated and aloof, whether there are any significant sexual problems or concerns which he may wish to express, the "masculinity" or "femininity" of his vocational interests, the nature and extent of any concerns which he may have about his health, the extent of his self-confidence and whether the front which he presents is real or, perhaps, bravado, whether his upbringing was fairly strict or lacking in discipline, whether he experiences feelings of guilt when he behaves aggressively toward others, and whether his orientation is pro-social or anti-social.

In fact, you can't ask a person that many questions about himself with getting to know him a little better, and my experience has been that, even in prison, most people will give you relatively straight answers to relatively straight questions. They may exaggerate a bit here-and-there, but they usually give a fairly accurate picture of where-they-are-at the time they do the test. This is not to say that the picture which a person presents of himself in responding to the MMPI is not highly susceptible to distortion should he care to do so, but most people don't; and furthermore, the questionnaire does contain a variety of validity scales which can provide the clinician with indications of response tendencies which may have influenced the individual's self-description, notably unconscious defensiveness and a tendency to give deviant responses, so that you can usually tell whether or not to accept what he says about himself at face value, or whether to accept what he says about himself with a grain of salt, or the whole bag. Which brings me to the main point of this paper, which is that the use of any so-called objective personality questionnaire does not give you license to turn your head off:

Rodgers (1972) has observed that: "A well-publicized strength of the MMPI is its empirical derivation and forming. This empiricism tempts the uninformed professional to assume that sophistication and interpretive skills are less important for this test than for other commonly used tests. Such unfortunately is not the case. The MMPI is a very complex psychometric instrument ... and can be a greater hazard in the hands of a naive interpreter than are tests which make no claim to prima facie validity and are not so seductively normed by quantified scores in a T score distribution" (p.244). The hazard involved is the same one which tempts people to think that empty gasoline drums are less dangerous than full gasoline drums. Because the test is referred to as "objective," there is a tendency to believe that less interpretive skill is required than is the case with other types of data.

Recently, I had a colleague tell me that he rarely uses the MMPI because what it tells him about his patients rarely agrees with his interview-based clinical impression. In fact, however, the MMPI will never tell you anything about a person. It doesn't stand up and yell, "This is schizophrenia". You may tell yourself some things about a person who has answered the questionnaire, but whether or not you will be right depends on whether or not you stop to think about what you are doing. Let's just run through that process briefly to see how it goes, and I hope to show you how such a process can be useful in teaching personality assessment.

There is a theory extant that psychologists are trained in science. Now, there is some controversy about just what "science" means, with the controversy centering around the extent to which experimental method must be invoked in the investigation of empirical events. But whatever this science which we are so quick to espouse involves, at the very least, it has to refer to the observation of events and attempts to explain them. And yet we typically fall down on both counts. First, few clinicians are competent observers, certainly not in the same league with Kraepelin. More of that later. Second, we don't do so well on interpretation either; and in this regard I would like to quote from Sheldon Korchin's recent text "Modern Clinical Psychology." Korchin (1976) cites the famous case of Theodor Reik (1948):

"One session at this time took the following course. After a few sentences about the uneventful day, the patient fell into a long silence. She assured me that nothing was in her thoughts. Silence from me. After many minutes she complained about a toothache. She told me that she had been to the dentist yesterday. He had given her an injection and then had pulled a wisdom tooth. The spot was hurting again. New and longer silence. She pointed to my bookcase in the corner and said, 'There's a book standing on its head.' Without the slightest hesitation and in a reproachful voice I said, 'But why did you not tell me that you had had an abortion?' (p.263). His inference was correct." (p.261)

In the same vein, a study by Margaret T. Singer illustrates what an astute clinician can do with Rorschach protocols in clinical research. "The ... case concerned the differentiation of ulcer patients from those with ulcerative colitis, two medical conditions for which psychodynamic correlates have been proposed. An earlier research study had reported that of the many individual Rorschach scores only the total number of responses reliably distinguished the two groups (Krasner and Kornreich, 1954). In the face of these negative findings, Singer did a blind sorting of the same protocols, on the basis of her extensive experience both with psychosomatic patients and with the

Rorschach. She predicted correctly in fifty out of fifty-four cases."
(Korchin, p.261). This degree of accuracy doesn't follow specifically
from the choice of the Rorschach, but from the application of Singer's
clinical acumen. The same type of accuracy should be expected of
clinicians using the MMPI as their data base.

Quoting again from Korchin (1976), "The essential task facing
the clinician is the synthesis of diverse and sometimes fragmentary
bits of information into a coherent picture of the individual. Toward
this end, interpretation is needed to fit the given facts together into
a meaningful and useful conceptual scheme that can account for
the patient's thoughts, feelings, and actions. In the multi-procedure,
multi-level model of clinical assessment, the available 'raw data'
include the clinician's first-hand observations, impressions, and
empathic reactions, the reactions of others as viewed by the patient
and/or reported to the clinician, the patient's self-description in
interviews and tests, his performance in test situations, both in
terms of idiosyncratic responses and scores or profiles which allow
comparison with others. With all this before him, the clinician must
develop hypotheses which encompass and make sense of as much of
the information as possible." (p. 261, 2). The same type of interpretive
magic as that illustrated by Reik and by Singer is available to all
experienced clinicians who will take the time to think about what
they are doing, and I have seen many cases of MMPI interpretation
similar to the above. However, interpretation is not the purpose of
this paper. My main interest has been in that part of the assessment
which is concerned with the observation of the empirical events that
serve as the basis for the psychologist's interpretive endeavours, and
in the development of a computer program which will facilitate a
detailed analysis of MMPI responses.

No matter how "objective" a personality test may be, all it is a
more-or-less standardized stimulus situation to which a subject has to
respond. In so responding, he may tell you something about himself
directly, and you are at liberty to make other inferences about him
as well. If he chooses to provide you with a self-description – that is,
if he doesn't chew up the questionnaire or answer sheet, or doesn't

tell you to stuff it in your ear – his self-description may be compared
with the self-descriptions of patients with a wide variety of diagnoses:
neurotics, psychotics, and character disorders. But first, you have to
do your scientific thing.

The MMPI is ultimately valid, as an indicator of something, and
your problem is to decide just what it is a valid indicator of. Assuming
that your tests are being machine-scored, the scored (and perhaps
analyzed) test which you get back from the computer is probably a
reasonably valid indicator of what was put into the computer, if they
didn't get the names mixed up, or something like that. What was
submitted to the computer is probably a reasonably valid indicator
of what was marked on the answer sheet, if there weren't too many
key-punching errors. And what was marked on the answer sheet is
probably fairly close to what the subject intended to mark, if he didn't
get the instructions mixed up, or lose his place, or answer randomly,
and assuming always that he can read well enough to make his
responses meaningful.

But let us assume for the moment that what you get back from
the computer is some representation of the subject's self-description.
That self-description is probably best thought of as "what the subject
wanted to tell us that he is like". Now, that does not imply either that
he knows what he is like, or that he is able to tell anybody what he
does know about himself, or even that he would want you to believe
what he does tell you about himself. So you never take anything at
face value unless you have some reason to feel that it is fairly safe to
do so.

So first you check the validity scores. Scale F is a measure of the
extent to which the subject has given responses which are infrequently
given by the normal population. Scores of 26 and above are likely to
have resulted from marking the responses at random. Scores of 21
are likely to reflect indiscriminant responding to say the least. And
anything above 17 has to be taken with a grain of salt. Scale K is a
measure of how well defended the individual is. Scores of 10-15 are
about average. Anything above that is well-defended and anything
below that is poorly-defended, with respect to the admission of

psychological problems. If validity scale scores are within reasonable limits, the person's self-description is probably fairly accurate. In any event, you are probably fairly safe in reporting on his self-description. That is, "just give me the facts, ma'am" and we can perhaps begin to speculate about what they mean afterwards. (I believe that it is very important to teach would-be clinicians to distinguish between facts and opinions, which is what any interpretation of those facts is. Even facts exist only with some degree of probability, but opinions are acknowledged to be not even of the same order of probability. They are much less likely to be correct and should be stated as opinions rather than facts).

Let us begin, therefore, by an examination of the facts. One of the most fruitful places to start making sense of what a subject has said about himself is to see what it was that he said about himself that made his responses similar to or different from the responses given by the patients on whom the original clinical scales were derived, partly because in doing so you will gain an insight into the characteristics of patients with these different diagnostic labels.

Content analysis of the Hypochondriasis Scale won't tell you very much about hypochondriasis except that it has something to do with physical health. Actually, hypochondriasis is characterized by a lack of emotional investment in the outside world and a focusing of attention on internal, bodily sensations, often with resultant anxiety. Hypochondriacs tend to be conflicted regarding dependency – they both seek and resent dependent relationships – but you won't find out about that from an examination of the items in the scale, which involve health concerns only, not because hypochondriacs don't endorse other kinds of items with sufficient frequency for their inclusion in the scale but, rather, because other kinds of items were arbitrarily eliminated in the final stage of the construction of this scale for the sake of having a scale which was composed of purely somatic items, although the original Hypochondriasis label was retained.

Examination of the content of the items which go to make up most of the other clinical scales, on the other hand, provides a valuable insight into the diagnostic groups from which they were empirically derived. The Depression Scale, for example, contains a number of items which are related to the denial of aggressive impulses – an idea with considerable theoretical support and of considerable theoretical implication – in addition to the mood-related items which one would expect to find in such a scale. The Hysteria Scale contains a group of items related to sociability, trust, and friendliness, and reflecting the well-known repressiveness of the hysterical population from which the scale was derived. The Psychopathic Deviate Scale was not derived from the responses of Psychopaths in the traditional Clecklian (1964) sense, as the name would seem to imply, but from a group of "small p" psychopaths, young criminals with a long history of minor delinquencies, whose behavior appeared poorly motivated and poorly concealed. Gilberstadt and Duker (1965) found that their high Pd Scale patients more closely fit the description of personality trait disturbance, aggressive type, and were characterized by irresponsibility, immaturity, impulsiveness, emotional instability, alcoholism, and low frustration tolerance resulting in assaultiveness. "They showed evidence of underlying insecurity, guilt, and self-depreciatory attitudes" (p.59). And this is not surprising when you consider that the bulk of the scale is made up of items which are related to family discord, feelings of being hard done by, rebelliousness, depression and guilt.

Scale 6, Paranoia, was derived from responses of patients judged to have paranoid symptoms. These individuals tend to be lacking in basic trust in themselves and others (frequently due to perceived rejection by parents), chronically angry at having been mistreated and the expectation that they are going to be mistreated again, and hypervigilant for censure. Slight elevations on this scale (T-scores within the 60-70 range) suggest interpersonal sensitivity and some personality rigidity. Such individuals are likely to be somewhat disillusioned with others and a bit self-righteous. As elevations on this scale increase above 70, however, it is noted that these individuals tend to become more touchy, stubborn, and difficult. They tend to be suspicious of the motives of others and may misinterpret the words and actions of others to support their attitude towards them. They are prone to brooding, harbouring grudges, and feeling that in some way they are not getting what is due to them. They often project their own negative feelings onto others and then rationalize their resistance or rebellion against them by claiming that they are only responding to other people's attitudes toward them. They are prone to keep themselves aloof, which reflects their fear of vulnerability, dependency, etc. Basic issues of distrust of self and others, fear of underlying dependency needs, and need for control in relationships (generated by relationships with cruel, sadistic, or rejecting parents) all need to be attended to in dealing with these individuals.

As the elevation on any scale increases, so does the likelihood that the individual has endorsed the overtly pathological items in the scale. Individuals rarely obtain a score of 80 or more on the Paranoia scale without endorsing overtly persecutory paranoid items. Persecutory paranoid reactions imply regression to both neurotic and psychotic levels, in which relationships with others are used as a forum in which to act out primitive sado-masochistic fantasies. The repression which normally serves as the paranoid individual's main defense against awareness of unacceptable impulses is impaired as he regresses to less mature levels of organization under stress. Rather than accepting in himself the strong, primitive impulses which have been stimulated in him and incorporated as a part of his own personality through identification with rejecting parent figures, and which might well threaten his personality integration if admitted to consciousness, he defends himself through denial and through projection of these traits onto selected others ("selected" others perhaps because his hypervigilance prevents him from admitting that he feels everybody is out to get him, but more likely because his denial of his own unacceptability prevents him from seeing the whole world as allied against him, since the scale, in addition to a large number of items of a paranoid nature, such as "Someone has it in for me," "I believe I am being plotted against," and "At times I hear so well it bothers me," contains a considerable number of items which I would characterize as reflecting an expectation that people behave morally. Thus an individual may be situationally paranoid as, for example, when he has just been admitted to prison and says that everybody is conspiring against him, or he may be more characterologically paranoid as when he allows that people are basically O.K. but it is just that that son-of-a-bitch is out to get him).

Psychasthenia is a category which, since this test was developed, has been dropped from the American Psychiatric Association diagnostic manual. Nevertheless, the scale retains some usefulness as a general measure of anxiety and ruminative self-doubt. It is mainly of interest in relation to the elevation on Scale 8, Schizophrenia.

Recall that the Schizophrenia scale was derived from the responses of groups of schizophrenic patients, whatever that means, and what it means in this case is that the diagnostic construct is defined by the items on the Schizophrenia scale in addition to any other kinds of criteria which may have been used to establish the diagnosis. Thus, "schizophrenicness" is a function of the items which make up the Sc scale: sensory and motor disturbances, social isolation, feelings of being hard done by, alienation from family, sadness and apathy, sexual problems, feelings of guilt, and problems in controlling thinking, emotions, and behaviour.

And finally, the Hypomania scale, composed of items related to sociability and ease, denial of inferiority, accelerated thinking, the use of excitement as a defense against depression, family discord, feelings of being hard done by, egocentrism, psychophysiological disturbance, restlessness, and emotionality. I tend to think of these characteristics as developing in opposition to the feelings of self-depreciation, and apathy, and sadness, and the inhibition of aggressive impulses, identified by the Depression scale, often within the context of a parental environment which provides conditional acceptance for the achievements required to meet the parents' own needs for esteem.

Now, I have referred to these Basic Clinical Scales by name as well as numbers, partly because doing so has given me an opportunity to show how you can use these diagnostically-labelled scales to begin to explicate the diagnostic "entities" which underlie them, and partly because I want to say a few words about the idea of diagnostic entities itself.

Neophyte clinicians have a tendency to reify, if not deify, diagnostic constructs. They need to be specifically taught that the main purpose of psychological assessment is understanding, not classification (and this is particularly true within the prison system). Diagnoses are constructs, not entities. And individuals with the same diagnosis may be less similar in many ways than individuals with different diagnoses. In fact, that is one more advantage to the use of the MMPI in teaching personality assessment. These clinical scales are most frequently elevated in combination, mainly because the underlying diagnostic groups are not entirely dissimilar from each other. Marks and Seeman (1963), for example, found that about 70% of their psychiatric patients were depressed and anxious; and in fact, we find depression and anxiety items in most of these scales. So it is unlikely that one scale will be elevated and the others within normal limits. If that does happen, you are away to the races. But even if several scales are elevated, there is no need to despair, for two reasons. First, the frequent occurrence of clinical scale elevations in combination and the marvelous array of patterns which typically emerge serves as a reminder that the diagnostic labels associated with these basic clinical scales may capture something important about the psychology of the individual who obtains a high score on one of these scales, but they don't begin to do justice to the complexity of personality. And second, the well-known empirical correlates of the various scale score elevations, singly or in combination, may provide an excellent basis for the beginning of a description of the individual in question but they can't compare to the understanding which is available to the clinician who will take the time to examine in detail just what the individual has actually indicated about himself.

For example, the modal description of the 4-9 personality might be somewhat as follows: "Individuals with high scores on both Scales 4 and 9 are generally extroverted rather than introverted. They tend to respond to obvious events in the world around them; they are not introspective by nature and do not appreciate this characteristic in others. Their reactions to people tend to be influenced by their feelings of the moment rather than by any studied or careful analysis either of their own emotions of those of others. They like to have lively and stimulating people around them. They readily accept praise and seek out people who give it, but when others impose standards of performance or criticize their behaviour, they are likely to reject them and may even turn against them. In many ways they seem immature, both intellectually and emotionally. They need immediate gratification and do not enjoy the delay of working toward long-term goals. They usually seek to influence others by their own efforts and personal charm rather than by logical arguments. In turn, they are more readily influenced by superficial appearance and short-term gain than by remote consequences. Heavy drinking and marital discord are the rule. Among adolescents, the 4-9 pattern is associated with both sexual and aggressive delinquencies and with prolific drug use."

The appropriateness of this description for a given individual, however, is bound to depend upon at least three factors: (1) the absolute and relative elevations of each of these two highest scales, (2) the items which he has endorsed, in each of these scales and others, in order to obtain this type of profile, and (3) the suitability or the appropriateness of the reference group from which this modal description was derived. That is, a high 4-9 is likely to be different from a low 4-9; and a difference of 10-15 scale score points between the two scales, in either direction, is likely to make some difference as well. Furthermore, it makes a difference whether Scale 4 is elevated by endorsement of items related to family discord, feelings of being hard done by, rebelliousness (possibly impulsiveness), by depression and guilt, or by some combination of the above; and it makes a difference whether Scale 9 is elevated by endorsement of items related to sociability and ease, denial of inferiority, or egocentrism. And finally, the delinquencies of 4-9 psychologists are likely to be less blatantly anti-social than the delinquencies of many other 4-9 groups, notably criminals. Most of the available modal descriptions were developed on hospitalized psychiatric patients and may not be appropriate to the population which you happen to be dealing with.

The student clinician, therefore, must be taught that there is no excuse for not looking at and thinking about the subject's responses, to see in what ways this particular individual is similar to and different from the individuals on which these basic clinical scales and subsequent code types were developed, regardless of how many well-turned phrases are available among the descriptive statements for the scale elevations which he may find. He can then present what information he has regarding the normative group whose profiles were similar to the one at hand, the ways in which this individual's self-description compares to that of the reference group, and his own speculation about what that might mean for this person, taking into account the extent to which the reference group comparison is appropriate, the likely validity of the subject's self-description, everything he knows about what people can he like, the probable effect of what he says in his psychological report, and anything else which comes to mind. And it is that point that you have become engaged in the process of personality assessment.

REFERENCES

Cleckley, H. The Mask of Sanity (4th ed.). Saint Louis, Mo.: Mosby, 1964

Gilberstadt, H., and Duker, J. A Handbook for Clinical and Actuarial MMPI Interpretation. Philadelphia: Saunders, 1965.

Gynther, M.D. Minnesota Multiphasic Personality Inventory. In O.K. Buros (Ed.), The Seventh Mental Measurements Yearbook (Vol. I). Highland Park, N.J.: Gryphon Press, 1972.

Korchin, S.J. Modern Clinical Psychology. New York: Basic Books, 1976.

Krasner, L., and Kornreich, M. Psychosomatic illness and projective tests. Journal of Projective Techniques, 1954, 18, 353-367.

Marks, P.A., and Seeman, W., The Actuarial Description of Abnormal Personality. Baltimore: Williams and Wilkins, 1963.

Marks, P.A., Seeman, W., and Haller, D.L. The Actuarial Use of the MMPI with Adolescents and Adults. Baltimore: Williams and Wilkins, 1974.

Reik, T. Listening with the Third Ear. New York: Farrar, Strauss, 1948.

Rodgers, D.A. Minnesota Multiphasic Personality Inventory. In O.K. Buros (Ed.), The Seventh Mental Measurements Yearbook (Vol. I). Highland Park, N.J.: Gryphon Press, 1972.

CHAPTER 7

An Introduction to Neuro-Linguistic Programming

In the early 20th century, physics was on the verge of becoming the first closed science. That is, some physicists, at least, believed that they knew all there was to know about the laws of the universe. Then came atomic physics and quantum mechanics, and we discovered that we really didn't know very much about the universe, after all.

What we now know is that the universe that we perceive is a fantasy. There may be (in fact, there probably is) a reality out there somewhere, but our only contact with it is through the energy which impinges on our sense organs and the way in which our brains structure that experience. The reality that we live in, on a day-to-day basis, is the reality that we construct in our own minds; it is composed of the pictures and sounds and tastes and smells and feelings that are formed in our brains from the sensory information which we receive through our visual, auditory, gustatory, olfactory and kinesthetic senses, plus the language that we use to structure those sensory experiences. We exist, for all time, in both an objective reality and a subjective reality.

Time itself exists for us only as memories of the past and fantasies of the future. The present moment, in which all time is experienced, is infinitely short but constantly shifting, the venturi through which the future pours into the past. The past exists for us only as we recall, in the present, the subjective reality – the sensory experiences and the language through which we structured them – that existed for us at the time our memories of those past events were created.

Because that experience was entirely subjective, and conditioned by who we were at the time, with whatever strengths and weaknesses we had at that time, it would have been different if we had been different. Fortunately, because the past exists for us only as we experience it in the present, it can become different for us if we can learn to experience it differently. And we can learn to experience it differently by reliving it in memory, with those personal resources that we have now but which we did not have then. This can have a profound effect on the way in which we experience not only our past but our present and future as well. It can, for example, change the way we experience those situations to which we have learned to respond with distress.

But before we demonstrate some of the procedures that have been developed by the NLP community to facilitate such change, let me tell you a bit about the history of this new and exciting cognitive behavioural approach. Probably the earliest reference to anything like Neuro-Linguistic Programming comes from the field of General Semantics, which was founded by Alfred Korzybski in 1933, with the publishing of his magnum opus, Science and Sanity. His observation that "the map is not the territory" was intended to remind us not to confuse perception (through which we create our subjective reality) with the objective reality which being perceived.

General semantics later became linguistics and transformational grammar. With a background in linguistics and some training in psychology, Richard Bandler, one of the cofounders of Neuro-linguistic Programming, had the great good fortune to serve as editor for some of Fitz Perls' work. In reading the work that he was editing, he began to say to himself, "Hey, I can do this." So he began to set up some Gestalt therapy sessions in Santa Cruz, in California, where he lived. These Gestalt sessions attracted the attention of a professor at the University of Santa Cruz by the name of John Grinder. So John and Richard got together, and one of the very first things that they did was to decide that, through this particular modelling process which Richard had been using, they could take and literally recreate anyone's behaviour. And they were interested, particularly, in modelling excellence, so that anyone could actually do whatever it was that was being modelled.

The first person that they began to study was Virginia Satir who, until her recent death, was the grandmother of family therapy. People would come to her and they would actually get well, as if by magic. Richard and John looked at what Virginia did, and they looked at her book, Conjoint Family Therapy, and they discovered a series of questions that she used to ask. This particular series of questions became the basis for the Meta Model (that is, a model of the client's model of the world, as reflected in language), which became Richard's M.A. thesis and was later published as The Structure of Magic, Volume I, which became one of the seminal writings in NLP. In it, they noted that, by the questions which she asked, Virginia Satir directed her clients to become more specific about their actual experiences, which served to bring them out of trance.

Now, Richard knew Gregory Bateson through Bateson's son, with whom he shared an interest in music. And while John and Richard were writing the second volume of The Structure of Magic, Bateson got in touch with them and told them that they should go and talk to Milton Erickson who, until his recent death, was the greatest medical hypnotist of this century. And what they discovered when they talked to Erickson was that he was doing just the opposite of what Satir had been doing.

They had been looking at Satir and had decided that, in order to get results in therapy, what you want to do is gain greater specificity in the client's representation of the world, so that the client restores the deletions, distortions, and generalizations which interfere with his ability to function effectively in the world. And then they discovered that Erikson was doing just the opposite. He used language patterns which were vague and ambiguous. So they had to make up another model, which they called the Milton Model. At that point they wrote the two volume set, Patterns in the Hypnotic Techniques of Milton H. Erickson, M.D.

About that same time, they began to develop the notion of representational systems. Way back in 1933, Alfred Korzybski has coined the phrase, 'The map is not the territory," to draw attention to the mistaken belief which most of us have that our internal representations of events are identical with the events themselves. Building on that foundation, Richard and John observed that different people draw their maps with different coloured pencils. Some people have an internal representational system that is primarily auditory in nature. The internal reality in which they live is constructed primarily of words. Others are primarily visual; the building blocks which they use to construct reality are pictures. Still others are primarily kinesthetic; and they think in terms of feelings. Furthermore, the individual's primary representational system tends to be reflected in the predicates which he uses. "Do you see what I mean?" "Can you hear what I am saying?" and "Does that feel right to you?" respectively.

As that was happening, John and Richard began to integrate into their thinking the behavioural psychology of Pavlov, and they began to talk about the process of anchoring in the book, Frogs into Princes, published in 1979, and using anchoring to change a person's history. That is, in the training being offered around that time, they began to take the notion of stimulus-response conditioning and applying it to the cognitive processes of human beings.

In 1980 they incorporated some work done by Carl Pribram. Pribram, along with Miller and Gallanter had written a book called Plans and The Structure of Behaviour, in which was outlined the notion of the TOTE, an acronym for test, operate, test, exit. When this notion was brought into NLP, the notion of cognitive strategies was born.

In 1982 a number of things happened. Richard and his wife, Leslie, went through a divorce, and John and Richard separated at roughly the same time. Richard moved to Hawaii, lived in Kona for a couple of years on the big island, hung out over there, fished and had fun; and along the way he went down and did a couple of seminars at Marshall University which were eventually transcribed and put into the book called Magic in Action, which came out in 1984. Magic in Action, while it wasn't an important book at the time, was one of the most important NLP books that have been written because, in it, Richard showed how he actually did therapy.

Then, in 1985, Richard dropped a major bombshell on the NLP community, a book called "An Insider's Guide to Submodalities." Prior to 1985, the NLP community and the world were aware of the various sensory modalities, but little attention had been paid to submodalities. Think of anything that you think of in pictures, for example, and you will see that it has a wide variety of properties, including location, size, distance, colour, intensity, and focus. Similarly, sounds can vary in location, volume, tone, tempo, timbre, cadence, inflection, and so on. Feelings can vary in intensity, duration, and so on. And it is through these submodality differences that we distinguish between the meanings which our representations of events have for us. In effect, it is these finer sensory distinctions which define the reality in which we live.

Currently[8] there is an explosion of publications in NLP, one of the most important of which is Time Line Therapy and the Basis of Personality, by Wyatt Woodsmall and Tad James, published in 1988. However, rather than tell you about timeline, a notion first proposed by William James almost a hundred years ago, I am going to demonstrate it to you, and it will be the basis of our first procedure for the treatment of anxiety.

---

8   This was probably written about 1990 for presentation at an Ontario Psychological Association convention.

CHAPTER 8

Women's Lib, Witchcraft, and Sex[9]
or Let Your Goddess Be Your Guide[10]

In an article entitled "Who said women are all bad? Almost everybody," Landsberg (1983) reported the opinions of women expressed by a number of Titans of Western Thought. Socrates is quoted as saying that "Woman is the source of all evil. Her love is to be dreaded more than the hatred of a man." Plato believed that "Those of the men ... who led a life of cowardice and injustice were suitably reborn as women." Aristotle felt that "We should regard the female as afflicted with natural defectiveness." Pythagoras believed that "There is a good principle which created order, light and man, and an evil principle which created chaos, darkness and women." Martin Luther observed that "God created Adam Lord of All Living Creatures, but Eve spoiled it all." Napoleon Bonaparte avowed that

---

9   This is a paper that I gave at the Clinical Division banquet during the Annual Convention of the Ontario Psychological Association in 1983. The convention was to be held on a Thursday, Friday, and Saturday in February. On the Wednesday preceding the convention, as I wandered through the convention hotel, Len Goldsmith, the president of the Clinical Division, asked me if I would speak at the Clinical Division banquet on Friday. I agreed to do so and returned to my office at the Ontario Correctional Institute to prepare a talk. Personally, I think that it is the best thing that I have ever written.

10   The subtitle is a substitute. Some people found the original tongue-in-cheek subtitle, "*How* to Fuck Your Way to the Top," offensive, even when it was explained that it should be read as "***How*** to Fuck Your Way to the Top," not "How to ***Fuck*** Your Way to the Top."

"Nature intended women to be our slaves ... they are our property ... just as a tree that bears fruit belongs to a gardener. What a mad idea to demand equality for women! Women are nothing but machines for producing children." Tolstoy said that we should "Regard the society of women as a necessary unpleasantness of social life, and avoid it as much as possible." And Freud said that "The great question that has never been answered and which I have not yet been able to answer, despite my thirty years of research into the feminine soul, is what does a woman want?" But the most telling quotation of all is from Kurt Vonnegut who said "Educating a beautiful woman is like pouring honey into a fine Swiss watch: Everything stops."

Certainly, the inferior position of women has existed for a long, long time, and there is some question as to whether women are even holding their own. In a recent article concerning changes in the status of women since the Second World War, Lipovenko (1983) reported as follows: "While the number of Canadian women working outside the home has grown rapidly since the post war years, there is 'depressingly little change in the kind of work they do,' says a federal report to be released today [21 February 1983]....

More than 70 per cent of women who work for pay are in clerical, service, sales, processing and fabricating jobs – and women are becoming more dominant in those traditionally female occupations, says the report for the Canadian Advisory Council on the Status of Women....

As of 1980, onethird of all working women do clerical work and half of them are concentrated in trade and service – the lowest paid industrial sectors, the report noted.

Since 1975, women have lost ground in two wellpaid occupations – teaching and jobs involving machines. There has been a significant drop in the number of fulltime teaching jobs going to women: new teaching jobs are going to men working fulltime and to women employed part-time....

Women's average annual earnings in 1979 (the most recent year for which data were available) were $7,673 compared to $14,981 for men, the report said." [11] It is within this context that I offer to women my advice on getting ahead in the world.

In classical clinical psychoanalysis, narcissistic character disorders were believed to be untreatable because of an impenetrable barrier to the establishment of any kind of transference relationship with the analyst. However, as this impenetrable barrier began to be penetrated by investigations into primitive internalized object relations and their role in the treatment of preOedipal conditions, it was found that this nihilistic belief was, in fact, far from valid. Actually, very strong transferences are established, but these strong transferences also induce strong countertransference reactions in the therapist, and these countertransference reactions tend to interfere with therapy. According to Searles (1979), "The analyst inevitably regresses in the course of the session and will experience the patient as being identified with the so called bad mother of the patient's past. The analyst will inevitably react to the patient as being a very disappointing and enraging unempathetic mother...." However, if the analyst properly understands rage and hate and other negative emotions, and particularly if he or she sees them as disintegration products caused by wounds to self-esteem, then it is sometimes possible to step out of these negative countertransference reactions or, alternatively, to metabolize them into insight when that is required. Proper use of these negative emotions enables the analyst to mirror the narcissistic character's emerging personality until the presymbolic stage of mental development is mastered and the client becomes able to appreciate the reality of the symbols involved in interpretation of his productions. When this occurs, the exhibitionistic-grandiose Self, which has finally been "heard" by its captive audience, can transform into more realistic self-esteem. This transformation heralds the second stage in the treatment of the narcissistic character disorder, in which

---

11   As a 2008 update, the gender gap in salaries was $ 0.71 for women for every $ 1.00 earned by men. The gender gap remains regardless of education. "Female high school graduates earn 27 percent less than male graduates. Female university graduates earn 16 percent less than male graduates." (The Toronto Star, September 17, 2008).

the client begins an introspective examination of and investment in the Self.

According to von Franz (1964, p. 162), "The Self can be defined as an inner guiding factor that is different from a conscious personality ... a regulating center that brings about a constant extension and maturing of the personality. But this larger, more nearly total aspect of the psyche appears first as merely an inborn possibility. It may emerge very slightly, or it may develop relatively completely during one's lifetime. How far it develops depends on whether or not the ego is willing to listen to the messages of the Self." And the narcissistic character (and each of us to the extent that we share narcissistic character traits) is absolutely terrified of discovering the Self, for fear that emotional interaction with the unconscious will result in personality disintegration and death. However, if the narcissistic character can summon sufficient courage to begin this self-exploration, he is most likely to find not eternal chaos but just the opposite, an inner reality that is both strong and dependable. In the process, however, the narcissistic character is brought face-to-face with a deeper schizoid level within himself, although one which is very different from that of the schizoid personality. In the latter case, the split-off Self is passive, and its energy content is easily drained. But there are schizoid dynamics that are symptomatic of a different kind of split-off Self, one which is intensely alive and exudes a sense of power, one which is connected to and sustained by the archetypal dimension of the Goddess, the feminine influence which dominated archaic cultures until it was suppressed by the development of a more patriarchal society.

When this schizoid dynamic appears, it is often indicated in dreams in the form of two children. These children are not exactly equals but, rather, one is more potent than the other, far more archetypal, "the true child of joy," while the other is more passive, more easily depressed, and more generally masochistic. The deeper child image, the child infused with joy, comes forth much less often than the other, usually slightly older child. Relating to either child is fraught with difficulty, for the masochistic child aspect of the emerging self induces strong sadistic feelings in the analyst while the joyful child stimulates the transference to become eroticized as the patient tests the feasibility of letting himself or herself be identified with the joyful child. Both have to be accepted in a caring, kinship sense, for when both these children can become integral parts of the personality, the patient gains not only the empathy associated with successful resolution of the depressive phase of child development but also the archetypal energies of the child of joy, a new awareness of the Goddess within, and a feminine force within the personality before which egocentric masculine grandiosity pales into insignificance.

Now, you may wonder what this has to do with women's lib, witchcraft, and sex. The answer is that few of us are likely to undergo the transforming power of psychoanalysis, so we have to find some other way to get in touch with the archetypal energies of the Goddess within; and witchcraft is one possible option. You may recall that in Greek mythology Zeus was king of the gods. He was married to Hera, and they had a son by the name of Ares who was the cruel and bloody god of war. When Ares went into battle, his sons Phobos (or fear) and Deimos (terror) prepared his chariot. There were also times, however, when Ares made love and not war; at least he managed to find time between battles to get together with Aphrodite (whom Botticelli reminds us rose from the sea foam on a scallop shell) for long enough to produce a son by the name of Eros, whom the Romans knew as Cupid. The love between Cupid and Psyche is one of the great love stories of all time, but it is more than just a love story. Psyche is the Greek word for "soul," and the deeper meaning of the story of Cupid and Psyche is that, while the soul may be condemned for a period of time to undergo misery and hardship, still, if it is faithful and true, it will eventually return to heaven and be reunited with love. However, this is not a love story, and I digress.

Although Zeus was married to Hera, he was as immoral as he was immortal, and he had many children by many different mates. The twins, Apollo and Artemis, he fathered on Latona, daughter of the Titans Coeus and Phoebe. Apollo was considered to be the god of the sun, and he later came to be associated with Lucifer because of a reference in Isaiah to Lucifer, son of the morning. Artemis was goddess of the moon, and she came to be associated with the Roman goddess Diana, and it is as Diana that she is most familiar to us today. Lucifer and Diana had an incestuous affair, and Diana gave birth to Aradia who eventually came down to earth and taught men and women the secrets of witchcraft. This, according to the legend, was because the church and the aristocracy were treating the poor with such cruelty that Diana felt they needed to be provided with some means of self-defense. In fact, the Church of the Middle Ages was truly becoming the Church Militant, flexing its muscles in the battle to suppress all nonChristian and nonpatriarchal expressions of religion. In particular, it wanted to suppress the Old Religion and the sexuality that was associated with it. The witch trials and the documents which supported them were, at one and the same time, like neurosis, both an expression of and a defense against the demonic in man and, in particular, against sexuality. But witchcraft was not easy to suppress. The persecution of witches lasted for almost 600 years and only came to an end when science began to supplant religion as the major guiding force in men's lives. And even then, witchcraft continued to be suppressed, only becoming legal again in England, for example, in the 1950's, probably in response to the increasing dissatisfaction with science as saviour in human affairs.

Now, I am not advocating a return to the primitive world of the past; but from time to time, I think about the story of the man who was clinically dead and then brought back to life. The first thing that he said was, "I have seen God, and She is black." And I wonder if, in man's creation of God in his own image, whether we may not have lost sight of the value of the Goddess within. And I wonder whether, in our espousal of science and achievement, we may not have abandoned living and being for advancement and doing. And it is not that the solution is necessarily to become involved in a return to witchcraft, but it is important to find some way to get in touch with the feminine within you.

So I come at last to the climax, my advice to women on how to get ahead in the world. Don't do it the way most men would do it. Don't get caught up in the North American business ethic. Don't mistake the stereotypic male for the masculine ideal. Don't be seduced by the ephemeral grandiosity of egocentric "power thrusting." Don't sell your birthright for a mess of pottage. Rather, consider the power of the archetypal Goddess, the Eternal Feminine. Put yourself in touch with the joyous child within you; and do it with panache; for if you do, no power on earth will be able to hold you back. And you'll go a long way, baby.

REFERENCES

Asimov, I., *Words from the Myths*. New York: New American Library, 1961.

Landsberg, M., Who said women are all bad? Almost everybody. Toronto: *The Toronto Star*, 17 February 1983.

Lipovenko, D., "Depressingly little" change in job status. Toronto: *The Globe & Mail*, 21 February 1983.

SchwartzSalent, N., *Narcissism and Character Transformation*. Toronto: Inner City Books, 1982.

Searles, H.P., "The Self in the countertransference." *Issues in Ego Psychology vol.2* (1979), no.2.

von Franz, M.L., The process of individuation. In C. G. Jung, *Man and His Symbols*. New York: Doubleday & Company, 1964.

CHAPTER 9

A Meditation on the Lord's Prayer

"Teach us how to pray," Jesus' disciples said to him (Luke 11:1), and he answered by teaching them the prayer that we call The Lord's Prayer:

Our Father who art in heaven, hallowed be thy name. Thy kingdom come. Thy will be done on earth, as it is in heaven. Give us this day our daily bread, and forgive us our trespasses, as we forgive those who trespass against us. And suffer us not to be led into temptation, but deliver us from evil. For thine is the kingdom, the power, and the glory, forever. Amen.

Many of us have learned to say this prayer without giving it a lot of thought. I invite you to consider it in a little more depth.

Our Father

God – "In the beginning God created the heavens and the earth." "All things exist and have their being in God." He is our Creator, Sustainer, and the source to which our borrowed dust returns.

God, you choose to reveal yourself to us, and we understand you to be omnipotent, omnipresent, omniscient, eternal and unchangeable, a morally perfect Being, righteous and loving. Your Son, Jesus, who lived in a very patriarchal society, spoke of you as Abba – Father.

In the Lord's Prayer, Jesus invites us to draw near to God, that loving spirit which is beyond human understanding, a holy mystery. However, while we may call God "Father," calling God "Father" does not mean that God is masculine. God is beyond all human categories; and none of our descriptions is adequate to encompass his majesty. Yet, Jesus teaches that we have a child-to-parent relationship with God; God sees us as if we were a daughter or a son. And we, on our part, can approach God in the familiar confident way a child approaches a loving parent. Nevertheless, God cannot yet be fully known by us.

Moses, is said to have spoken to God face-to-face: "If there is a prophet among you, I, the Lord, make myself known to him in a vision; I speak to him in a dream. Not so with my servant Moses; He is faithful in all my house. I speak with him face to face."

Others have found that God speaks to them through nature, as illustrated y Bliss Carman's poem, Vestigia (see On Being Perfect, above).

Some hermits, withdrawing from the world, claimed to have found God within their inmost souls.

Buddhists don't teach a personal God but, in quieting their minds, some have experienced a love that permeates the universe; and we remember that God is that love.

The Muslim mystic, Rumi, wrote: "A seeker knocked at the door of the beloved – God – and a voice from inside asked: 'Who is it?' The seeker answered 'It is I'; and the voice said: 'In this house there is no You and I' (and I note the reference to the abnegation of duality, but that is a topic for some other day). The door remained locked. Then the seeker went into solitude, fasted and prayed and, later, returned and again knocked at the door. Again the voice asked: 'Who is it?' Now the believer answered: 'It is You.' Then the door opened."

Certainly a mystery, but perhaps that is what is meant by God being omnipresent.

who art in heaven

In the King James translation of the bible, this is given as "which art in heaven." In Joseph Smith's Inspired Version, this phrase is given as "who art in heaven." The New Jerusalem translation avoids the distinction, the choice between the personal "who" and the somewhat more impersonal "which," by simply saying as "Our Father in heaven."

And where is heaven? Metaphorically, it is above us, and we look up to his perfection, as in the old saying, "Ah, but a man's reach should exceed his grasp, or what's a heaven for?" But in another sense, it is around us and potentially within us, just as God is omnipresent, around us and within us.

Hallowed be Thy name.

"Hallowed" meaning "holy." "May your name be kept holy." By implication, "You shall not take the name of the Lord thy God in vain." I pray that we may not blunt our spiritual experience with a casual attitude toward our Heavenly Parent.

In the Bible, God is referred to by many names. *God, may we always honour your name and hold it sacred, Elohim (majestic ruler over all), Jehovah (master of the universe), Adonai (Lord of lords), El Shaddai (who nurtures His people as a mother nurtures her child), El Olam (everlasting and unchangeable), Jehovah Jireh (who provides for our needs), Jehovah Rapha (Healer of your people), Jehovah Nissa (our banner who gives us hope in battle), El Qanna (who asks that we put him first in our lives), Jehovah Mekoddishkem (who sets his believers apart and makes them holy), Jehovah Shalom (Lord of Peace, of comfort and strength), Jehovah Sabaoth (Lord of hosts, our leader in battle), Jehovah Raah (our shepherd, who nourishes and protects, and rest for our weary souls), Jehovah Tsidkenu (righteous ruler), Jehovah Shammah (omnipresent in time of need).*

Thy kingdom come

"Kingdom" is not a metaphor with which I am comfortable; although I suppose that might just be pride talking. Nevertheless, I feel that thinking of God as king is even somewhat demeaning. For me, my God has always been so much more than that.

Origen, one of the early church fathers, has said that 'The kingdom of God is within us,' on our lips and in our hearts. In St. Luke (17:21) says that "…anyone who prays that the kingdom of God may not delay its coming is praying that it may be consolidated, extended, and reach its fullness within him[self]." And in St. Paul's letter to the Romans (Rom 14:17, NIV), we read "For the kingdom of God is righteousness, peace and joy in the Holy Spirit." *Oh, Lord, you dwell in all who recognize you as their God and abide by your spiritual laws. We pray that you will guide us as we try to follow the teachings of your Son, transforming this secular world into one in which your commandments are not only obeyed but embraced.*

Thy will be done on Earth, as it is in heaven.

In the third chapter of Genesis (in Joseph Smith's "inspired Version"), we read:

[Gen 3:1] And I, the Lord God, spake unto Moses, saying, That Satan whom thou hast commanded in the name of mine Only Begotten, is the same which was from the beginning;

[Gen 3:2] And he came before me, saying, Behold I, send me, I will be thy Son, and I will redeem all mankind, that one soul shall not be lost, and surely I will do it; wherefore, give me thine honor.

[Gen 3:3] But behold, my beloved Son, which was my beloved and chosen from the beginning, said unto me: Father, thy will be done, and the glory be thine forever.

[Gen 3:4] Wherefore, because that Satan rebelled against me, and sought to destroy the agency of man, which I, the Lord God, had given him; and also that I should give unto him mine own power; by the power of mine Only Begotten I caused that he should be cast down; and he became Satan.

[Gen 3:5] Yea, even the devil, the father of all lies, to deceive, and to blind men, and to lead them captive at his will, even as many as would not hearken unto my voice.

And the Book of Mormon offers the following insight:

[2 Ne 1:111] And now, behold, if Adam had not transgressed, he would not have fallen; but he would have remained in the garden of Eden.

[2 Ne 1:112] And all things which were created, must have remained in the same state which they were, after they were created; and they must have remained for ever, and had no end.

[2 Ne 1:113] And they would have had no children; wherefore, they would have remained in a state of innocence, having no joy, for they knew no misery; doing no good, for they knew no sin.

[2 Ne 1:114] But behold, all things have been done in the wisdom of him who knoweth all things.

[2 Ne 1:115] Adam fell, that men might be; and men are, that they might have joy.

[2 Ne 1:116] And the Messiah cometh in the fullness of time, that he may redeem the children of men from the fall.

Lord, we look forward to our own redemption, as we sing: "And as we hope for heaven, make earth a heaven below."

Give us this day our daily bread

In John 6:32-35 (NAS), we read that Jesus said to his followers, "Truly, truly, I say to you, it is not Moses who has given you the bread out of heaven, but it is My Father who gives you the true bread out of heaven. For the bread of God is that which comes down out of heaven, and gives life to the world." They said therefore to Him, "Lord, evermore give us this bread." Jesus said to them, "I am the bread of life; he who comes to Me shall not hunger, and he who believes in Me shall never thirst."

In the sixth chapter of Matthew, Jesus, speaking to his disciples, is reported to have said:

[Mat 6:25] And, again I say unto you, go ye into the world, and care not for the world; for the world will hate you, and will persecute you, and will turn you out of their synagogues.

[Mat 6:26] Nevertheless, ye shall go forth from house to house, teaching the people; and I will go before you.

[Mat 6:27] And your heavenly Father will provide for you, whatsoever things ye need for food, what ye shall eat; and for raiment, what ye shall wear or put on.

[Mat 6:28] Therefore I say unto you, take no thought for your life, what ye shall eat, or what ye shall drink; nor yet for your bodies, what ye shall put on. Is not the life more than meat, and the body than raiment?

[Mat 6:29] Behold the fowls of the air, for they sow not, neither do they reap, nor gather into barns; yet your heavenly Father feedeth them. Are ye not much better than they? How much more will he not feed you?

[Mat 6:30] Wherefore take no thought for these things, but keep my commandments wherewith I have commanded you.

[Mat 6:31] For which of you by taking thought can add one cubit unto his stature.

[Mat 6:32] And why take ye thought for raiment? Consider the lilies of the field, how they grow; they toil not, neither do they spin.

[Mat 6:33] And yet I say unto you, that even Solomon, in all his glory, was not arrayed like one of these.

[Mat 6:34] Therefore, if God so clothe the grass of the field, which today is, and to-morrow is cast into the oven, how much more will he not provide for you, if ye are not of little faith.

In fact, of all God's children, we are the most fortunate:

"If you have food in the refrigerator, clothes on your back, a roof overhead and a place to sleep … you are richer than 75% of this world.

If you have money in the bank, in your wallet, and spare change in a dish someplace … you are among the top eight percent of the world's wealthy.

If you woke up this morning with more health than illness … you are more blessed than the million who will not survive this week.

If you have never experienced the danger of battle, the loneliness of imprisonment, the agony of torture, or the pangs of starvation… you are ahead of 500 million people in the world.

If you can attend a church meeting without fear of harassment, arrest, torture, or death … you are more blessed than three billion people in the world.

If you hold up your head with a smile on your face and are truly thankful … you are blessed because, while the majority can, but most do not.

If you can hold someone's hand, hug them or even touch them on the shoulder, you are blessed because you can offer healing touch.

If you can read, you are more blessed than over two billion people in the world that cannot read at all."

But: "Man shall not live by bread alone, but by every word that proceeds out of the mouth of God." We should turn to you, Heavenly Father, for spiritual guidance as well as for our physical wants and needs. Not for our bodies alone, then, do we pray, but for our very souls. Let us truly be the body of Christ Jesus, the tools of your hands, bringing justice and peace to a world in need.

and forgive us our trespasses

The royal feast was done. The king sought some new sport to banish care and, to his jester, cried, "Sir, Fool, kneel now and make for us a prayer."

The jester doft his cap-and-bells, and stood, the mocking court before. They did not see the bitter smile behind the painted grin he wore.

He bowed his head and bent his knee upon the monarch's silken stool. His pleading voice arose, "Oh, Lord, be merciful to me, a fool.

These clumsy feet, still in the mire, go crushing blossoms without end; These hard, well-meaning hands we thrust among the heartstrings of a friend."

The unkind word we might have kept, who knows how sharp it pierced and stung? The word we had not sense to say, who knows how grandly it had rung.

Our faults no tenderness should ask. The chastening stripes must cleanse them all. But for our follies, oh, in shame before the eyes of heaven we fall."

The room was hushed. In silence rose the king, and sought his gardens cool. His pleading voice arose, "Oh, Lord, be merciful to me, a fool."

"Dear Lord and Father of mankind, forgive our foolish ways; re-clothe us in our rightful mind, in purer lives thy service find, in deeper reverence, praise.

Drop thy still dews of quietness, till all our strivings cease; take from our souls the strain and stress, and let our ordered lives confess the beauty of thy peace.

Breathe through the heats of our desire thy coolness and thy balm; let sense be dumb, let flesh retire; speak through the earthquake, wind, and fire, O still, small voice of calm!"

Let us start each day anew, then, Lord, believing in hope that we may yet heed your will.

as we forgive those who trespass against us.

In the 18th chapter of the gospel according to St, Matthew, we read:

[Mat 18:21] Then came Peter to him and said, Lord, how oft shall my brother sin against me, and I forgive him? Till seven times?

[Mat 18:22] Jesus said unto him, I say not unto thee, until seven times; but until seventy times seven.

[Mat 18:23] Therefore is the kingdom of heaven likened unto a certain king, who would take account of his servants.

[Mat 18:24] And when he had begun to reckon, one was brought unto him who owed him ten thousand talents.

[Mat 18:25] But forasmuch as he had not to pay, his lord commanded him to be sold, and his wife, and children, and all that he had, and payment to be made.

[Mat 18:26] And the servant besought him, saying, Lord, have patience with me, and I will pay thee all.

[Mat 18:27] Then the lord of that servant was moved with compassion, and loosed him, and forgave him the debt. The servant, therefore, fell down and worshipped him.

[Mat 18:28] But the same servant went out, and found one of his fellow-servants which owed him a hundred pence; and he laid hands on him, and took him by the throat, saying, Pay me that thou owest.

[Mat 18:29] And his fellow-servant fell down at his feet, and besought him, saying, Have patience with me, and I will pay thee all.

[Mat 18:30] And he would not; but went and cast him into prison, till he should pay the debt.

[Mat 18:31] So when his fellow-servants saw what was done, they were very sorry, and came and told unto their lord all that was done.

[Mat 18:32] Then his lord, after that he had called him, said unto him, O thou wicked servant! I forgave thee all that debt, because thou desiredst me; shouldest not thou also have had compassion on thy fellow-servant, even as I had pity on thee?

[Mat 18:33] And his lord was wroth, and delivered him to the tormentors, till he should pay all that was due unto him.

[Mat 18:34] So likewise shall my heavenly Father do also unto you, if ye from your hearts forgive not every one his brother their trespasses.

And suffer us not to be led into temptation

God, we know that your purposes are beyond our understanding.

In the story of Job, for example, God allowed Satan to test Job; and Job's friends sought to explain to Job why he was being afflicted – You must have been punishing him because of his sins. Elihu says, for example,

[Job 36:5] Behold, God is mighty, and despiseth not any; he is mighty in strength and wisdom.

. . .

[Job 36:11] If they obey and serve him, they shall spend their days in prosperity, and their years in pleasures.

[Job 36:12] But if they obey not, they shall perish by the sword, and they shall die without knowledge.

. . .

[Job 38:1] Then the Lord answered Job out of the whirlwind, and said,

[Job 38:2] Who is this that darkeneth counsel by words without knowledge?

[Job 38:3] Gird up now thy loins like a man; for I will demand of thee, and answer thou me.

[Job 38:4] Where wast thou when I laid the foundations of the earth? declare, if thou hast understanding.

[Job 38:5] Who hath laid the measures thereof, if thou knowest? or who hath stretched the line upon it?

[Job 38:6] Whereupon are the foundations thereof fastened? or who laid the cornerstone thereof;

[Job 38:7] When the morning stars sang together, and all the sons of God shouted for joy?

[Job 38:8] Or who shut up the sea with doors, when it brake forth, as if it had issued out of the womb?

. . .

[Job 38:11] And said, Hitherto shalt thou come, but no further; and here shall thy proud waves be stayed?

[Job 38:12] Hast thou commanded the morning since thy days; and caused the dayspring to know his place;

...

[Job 38:16] Hast thou entered into the springs of the sea? or hast thou walked in the search of the depth?

[Job 38:17] Have the gates of death been opened unto thee? or hast thou seen the doors of the shadow of death?

[Job 38:18] Hast thou perceived the breadth of the earth? declare if thou knowest it all.

...

[Job 38:31] Canst thou bind the sweet influences of Pleiades, or loose the bands of Orion?

[Job 38:32] Canst thou bring forth Mazzaroth in his season? [i.e., the various signs of the zodiac] or canst thou guide Arcturus with his sons?

[Job 38:33] Knowest thou the ordinances of heaven? canst thou set the dominion thereof in the earth?

[Job 38:34] Canst thou lift up thy voice to the clouds, that abundance of waters may cover thee?

[Job 38:35] Canst thou send lightnings, that they may go, and say unto thee, Here we are?

...

[Job 39:9] Will the unicorn be willing to serve thee, or abide by the crib?

[Job 39:10] Canst thou bind the unicorn with his band in the furrow? or will he harrow the valleys after thee?

...

[Job 40:1] Moreover the Lord answered Job, and said,

[Job 40:2] Shall he that contendeth with the Almighty instruct him? he that reproveth God, let him answer it.

[Job 40:3] Then Job answered the Lord, and said,

[Job 40:4] Behold, I am vile; what shall I answer thee? I will lay mine hand upon my mouth.

[Job 40:5] Once have I spoken; but I will not answer; yea, twice; but I will proceed no further.

[Job 40:6] Then answered the Lord unto Job out of the whirlwind, and said,

[Job 40:7] Gird up thy loins now like a man; I will demand of thee, and declare thou unto me.

[Job 40:8] Wilt thou also disannul my judgment? wilt thou condemn me, that thou mayest be righteous?

[Job 40:9] Hast thou an arm like God? or canst thou thunder with a voice like him?

[Job 40:10] Deck thyself now with majesty and excellency; and array thyself with glory and beauty.

[Job 40:11] Cast abroad the rage of thy wrath; and behold everyone that is proud, and abase him.

[Job 40:12] Look on everyone that is proud, and bring him low; and tread down the wicked in their place.

[Job 40:13] Hide them in the dust together; and bind their faces in secret.

[Job 40:14] Then will I also confess unto thee that thine own right hand can save thee.

...

[Job 42:1] Then Job answered the Lord, and said,

[Job 42:2] I know that thou canst do everything, and that no thought can be withholden from thee.

[Job 42:3] Who is he that hideth counsel without knowledge? therefore have I uttered that I understood not; things too wonderful for me, which I knew not.

[Job 42:4] Hear, I beseech thee, and I will speak; I will demand of thee, and declare thou unto me.

[Job 42:5] I have heard of thee by the hearing of the ear; but now mine eye seeth thee;

[Job 42:6] Wherefore I abhor myself, and repent in dust and ashes.

[Job 42:7] And it was so, that after the Lord had spoken these words unto Job, the Lord said to Eliphaz the Temanite, My wrath is kindled against thee, and against thy two friends; for ye have not spoken of me the thing that is right, as my servant Job hath.

We hear you, Lord: No man has perfect understanding and none can rightly claim to apologize for you.

We acknowledge an evil spirit in opposition to you, therefore, loving spirit. May it always be Your will for us that we heed, that we may be saved from our sins. And if we are tempted, Lord, we know that it is because you have given us the gift of choosing between good and evil, and we thank you, Lord, for the gift of thy son, Jesus, that we have his example to follow.

"And I said to the man who stood at the gate of the year, 'Give me a light, that I may tread safely into then unknown.' And he replied: 'Go out into the darkness and put your hand into the Hand of God. That shall be to you better than light and safer than a known way.'

So, I went forth, and finding the Hand of God, trod gladly into the night. And He led me towards the hills and the breaking of the day in the lone East.

So, heart, be still: What need our little life, our human life, to know, if God hath comprehension?"

Send us forth, then, almighty God, to show to our world the teachings of your Son, Jesus, our Saviour, that we may be saved from our sins.

But deliver us from evil

And the answer is:
Here I am, Lord. Is it I, Lord? I have heard you calling in the night.
I will go, Lord, if you lead me. I will hold your people in my heart.

For Thine is the kingdom

As is right, victorious King: The world is yours and everything in it.
Glory be to you, Master of the Universe, who nurtures your people as a mother
nurtures her child.

We are yours, Lord, the children of your hand, as well as your hands
here on earth. May we indeed make earth a heaven below. Let your kingdom
come, first of all in our own souls, that we may begin to realize it in our
communities, and then throughout the world.

And the power

"O Lord my God, when I in awesome wonder,
Consider all the works Thy hands have made,
I see the stars, I hear the rolling thunder,
Thy power throughout the universe displayed.

Then sings my soul, My Saviour God to Thee,
How great Thou art, How great Thou art.
Then sings my soul, My Saviour God to Thee,
How great Thou art, How great Thou art."

I like to think of Jesus as God's love and power incarnate:

"Here is a man who was born in an obscure village, the child of a peasant woman. He worked in a carpenter shop until he was thirty, and then for three years He was an itinerant preacher. He never wrote a book. He never held an office. He never owned a home. He never had a family. He never went to college. He never put His foot inside a big city. He never traveled two hundred miles from the place where he was born. He never did one of the things that usually accompany greatness. He had no credentials but Himself. He had nothing to do with this world except the naked power of His divine manhood.

While still a young man, the tide of popular opinion turned against Him. His friends ran away. One of them denied Him. He was turned over to His enemies. He went through the mockery of a trial. He was nailed to a cross between two thieves. His executioners gambled for the only piece of property He had on earth while He was dying -- and that was His coat. When He was dead, He was taken down and laid in a borrowed grave through the pity of a friend.

Nineteen wide centuries have come and gone, and today He is the centerpiece of the human race and the leader in the column of progress. I am far within the mark when I say that all the armies that ever marched, and all the navies that ever were built, and all the parliaments that ever sat, and all the kings that ever reigned, put together have not affected the life of man upon this earth as powerfully as has that One solitary life." (James A. Francis) a man or, as my Jewish friends would say, a true mensch.

> And I think of that hymn, "Freely, freely":
> "God forgave my sin in Jesus' name;
> I've been born again in Jesus' name;
> And in Jesus' name I come to you
> To share his love as he told me to.
> All power is given in Jesus' name,
> In earth and heaven in Jesus';
> And in Jesus' name I come to you
> To share his power as he told me to."

And the glory

> *"The heavens herald your glory, O God, and the skies display your handiwork.*
> *Day after day they tell their story, and night after night they reveal the depth of their understanding.*
> *Without speech, without words, without even an audible voice,*
> *Their cries echo through all the world, and their message reaches the ends of the earth.*
> *Your law, Adonai, is perfect; it refreshes the soul.*
> *Your rule is to be trusted; it gives wisdom to the naive.*
> *Your purposes, God, are right; they gladden the heart.*

Your command is clear; it gives light to the eyes.
Holding you in awe, Adonai, is purifying; it endures.
Your decrees are steadfast, and all of them are just."

Forever,

Yes, El Olan, everlasting Father, for time without end.

Amen.

CHAPTER 10

Prelude to the Energy Therapies

Each person is a product of his or her heredity and environment. Each of us is born with a certain potential, and our ability to reach that potential is then either supported or not by the experiences that we encounter while growing up. Some of those experiences are positive and encourage us to reach our potential, and some are negative and discourage us from doing so.

Each of our experiences is remembered at some level, some consciously and some unconsciously. Memories of positive experiences have one or more positive emotional feelings attached to them, while memories of negative emotional experiences have one or more negative emotional feelings attached to them. These negative emotional feelings fall into three main categories: sadness, anxiety or fear, and anger.

Your positive, life-affirming experiences and your negative, unsupportive ones affect your view of yourself, of others, of the world in general, and even your relationship with God. That is, your experiences are likely to be accompanied by some kind of decision-making process, since it is as a result of your experiences that you decide what you are like, what others are like, and so on.

Negative experiences – those that generate memories which have a negative emotional charge attached to them – are likely to have been accompanied by decisions that limit you in some way. So then we come to the crux of the matter (where the rubber hits the road, so to speak):

If you always think the way you've always thought,
You'll always feel the way you've always felt;
And if you always feel the way you've always felt,
You'll always do what you've always done;
And if you always do what you've always done,
You'll always get what you've always got.
If nothing changes, nothing changes.

And that is okay if you are completely satisfied with the way things are going for you. If not, then it is time to let go of any negative emotions that may have become attached to the experiences you had in your past, and any limiting decisions as well, so that you can realize your fullest potential.

This is not to say that all negative emotions begin with negative thinking. Not at all. There are actually two routes to follow to become distressed. Both of these routes to distress begin with some event, which is then followed by either physiological arousal or negative thinking. The first is the "conditioned emotional arousal" route, which works as follows:

Event –> physiological arousal –> "negative"[12] thinking –> distress (i.e., anxiety, anger or sadness[13])

The second route to distress, *and the one which is much more common,* is the primarily cognitive route, which works as follows:

Event –> "negative" thinking –> physiological arousal –> distress

Please note that in each case, for distress to occur, both physiological arousal and negative thinking must be

---

12 "Negative" thinking merely refers to thinking that is supportive of becoming upset.

13 In the case of sadness, the physiological "arousal" may rebound to become physiological underarousal or suppression.

present. This suggests two particular approaches to treatment. The first, Systematic Desensitization, targets the physiological arousal; the second, Rational Emotive Therapy (RET), targets the negative thinking. Let me give you a bit of background on them:

In 1958, a psychiatrist by the name of Joseph Wolpe published a book entitled *Psychotherapy by Reciprocal Inhibition* in which he described a learning-based deconditioning procedure known as Systematic Desensitization. In essence, it involves teaching the client to relax and then, while relaxed, to approach the trigger stimulus (event) at a rate which is slow enough for the client to be able to maintain the relaxation. Assuming that the event is not currently harmful, this results in the eventual pairing of relaxation and the event, which teaches the body/mind that its proper response to that particular kind of trigger stimulus is relaxation rather than arousal. That is, the client learns *at a gut level* that there is no need to get "all cranked up" about that particular kind of event. Hence, no more distress!

Shortly afterwards, Albert Ellis and Robert Harper published a book entitled *A Guide to Rational Living* in which they described a cognitively-based approach to treatment in which the client is taught to challenge his or her negative thinking on the grounds that it is erroneous or non-rational – based on such erroneous beliefs, for example, as the belief that it is *necessary* (as opposed to desirable) to be unfailingly perfect or the belief that it is *necessary* to be universally loved – since erroneous beliefs put the client in conflict with the laws of the universe and invariably contribute to his or her becoming distressed ("shooting oneself in the foot," as it were).

Albert Ellis (*A New Guide to Rational Living*, 1975) identifies a number of different "negative" thoughts that, because they put the individual in conflict with the laws of the universe, contribute to his or her distress. These thoughts – beliefs really – always include value judgements or evaluations of the way things are:

1. I don't get the love that I want to get, and I <u>should</u> get the love that I want.

2. I am not perfect, and I <u>must</u> be perfect (or at least close enough to it that people can't criticize me).
3. Certain people are bad and <u>should</u> be punished.
4. The world is not the way I want it to be, and it <u>should</u> be.
5. External events cause most human misery and <u>must</u> be controlled in order to create happiness and avoid sorrow.
6. The unknown is potentially dangerous, so it <u>should</u> be feared.
7. Taking responsibility for what happens is scary and <u>should</u> be avoided.
8. You can't always know what is the right thing to do, so you <u>should</u> turn your life over to someone or something stronger than yourself (Kaufmann calls this "Decidophobia," the fear of making fateful decisions).
9. The past determines the present, so I <u>should</u> not be held responsible for what I do with my life.
10. Leisure is more precious than any other activity and <u>should</u> be sought out whenever possible.

Such irrational beliefs inevitably lead to frustration, disappointment and distress; whereas challenging these irrational beliefs and substituting more realistic beliefs for them leads to harmony and contentment.

With those treatment approaches as background, we may then approach the energy therapies. Quoting from a book by James Durlacher (Freedom From Fear Forever, 1994):

"Some five thousand years ago the Chinese began observing a phenomenon of energy in the body that they eventually called CHI (pronounced chee), which means 'life force.' ...the energy seemed to flow along particular lines or pathways [which they] called meridians. They found there were points along these energy meridians that, when stimulated, could balance or transfer energies to make them flow freely and evenly, restoring normal function to various parts of the body. ... It was also observed that each of the meridians had a specific emotion connected with it, and that if a person had an over or under abundance of that emotion, balancing the energies could restore the person's normal emotional balance." (pp. 39-40)

In 1966, a chiropractor by the name of George Goodheart found that:

> "...another way of stimulating the various points of the energy meridians was to percuss (tap) the point with the finger tip. He described the procedure as a way to relieve pain and presented his results in 1979 at the annual summer meeting of the newly formed (1974) International College of Applied Kinesiology." (p. 41)

Shortly afterwards, a psychologist by the name of Roger Callahan contacted George Goodheart, took the applied kinesiology training, and began to adapt applied kinesiology to psychological problems. In 1981, he published a paper called "A Rapid Treatment for Phobias," and Thought Field Therapy was born.

Now, as was previously mentioned, the Chinese found that specific meridians were associated with specific emotions. Thought Field Therapy is based on the premise that the cause of *all* negative emotions is a disruption in the body's energy system, and that these negative emotions can be eliminated by tapping on various (acupressure) points on the energy meridians to restore the energy balance ***while thinking of the disturbance***, just as proposed in Chinese medicine so many years ago. That in itself was hardly original; however, Callahan does seem to have added one important piece to the puzzle of emotional disturbance and its treatment, and that is the idea of Psychological Reversal. It was his experience that tapping at certain places on the energy meridians was successful in rapidly eliminating emotional disturbances in approximately 60% of cases. In trying to understand why the success rate wasn't higher, he came to a couple of conclusions: first, that progress was being blocked by a kind of low-self-esteem-related self-sabotage and, second, that this self-sabotage – which he called "psychological reversal" – could be eliminated, at least temporarily, by having the patient say "I accept myself even though I have this problem" (stating the specific problem that the client consciously wants to eliminate) *while tapping or rubbing on certain energy-system-related points on the body.*

Callahan began offering training in this new method, which he called Thought Field Therapy (on the grounds that "the trauma is encoded in the Thought Field"), and an engineer by the name of Gary Craig was one of the first people to invest in that training. However, Craig disagreed with Callahan on a few basic points and is now promoting a variation of Callahan's Thought Field Therapy which he calls Emotional Freedom Technique (www.emofree.com). The main differences are as follows:

Callahan (TFT) says that disturbances (perturbations) in the thought field function as triggers for the physiological, neurological, hormonal, chemical and cognitive events which result in the experience of specific negative emotions; and that a perturbation and the negative emotion that it controls can be eliminated by tapping at particular points on the energy meridian(s) while attuned to the thought field associated with that particular negative emotion. Callahan (TFT) determines the location and the tapping sequence by various diagnostic procedures or uses algorithms that are likely to work for specific problems. Craig (EFT) says that the above may be true but that, if you routinely correct for any potential psychological reversal and then tap on enough meridians in any order, you will eliminate the disturbance regardless of the kind of emotional problem. The standard EFT procedure simply uses the more common tapping points starting at the top and working your way down the body (upper body only), and repeats the process until the problem is eliminated. This method is not universally effective but it does tend to work in about eighty-five to ninety percent of cases; and when it does work, the effects are very dramatic.

Callahan Tapping Procedures Instructions

1. **Recall the most emotionally-charged example of the situation.** If there is more than one emotion associated with that situation, you should:

   a. **deal with one emotion at a time**, and
   b. **finish with that emotion before going on with the next one.**

   As a general rule, you might focus on shock/fear, then pain/hurt, then anger/rage, and so on.

2. Muscle test while asking, "Do you want to get rid of the distress associated with this situation?" and "Is it all right to get rid of it now?" If the answer is, "No," the person is "psychologically reversed" (usually there is a limiting belief of some kind). You can temporarily disconnect the reversal by doing "reverse tapping" (Reverse tapping involves tapping the outer edge of the hand between the little finger and the wrist -- about where you would do a karate chop -- while saying, "I accept myself even though I have this problem," three times).

3. **Associate into the memory, or focus on the pain itself. Then step back out and rate the distress** (You can substitute any emotion) on the Distress Scale (Anyone at the 10+ level can expect to feel worse before they feel better).

THE DISTURBANCE SCALE

10+   I feel numb.
10. The disturbance is as bad as it could be. It is more than I can stand.
9.   The disturbance is almost intolerable.
8.   The disturbance is very severe.

7. The disturbance is severe.

6. The disturbance is very uncomfortable.

5. The disturbance is uncomfortable, but I can tolerate it.

4. The disturbance is noticeable and bothersome, but I can deal with it.

3. The disturbance is slight, and I have it under control.

2. I am rather calm and quite relaxed, and feel no particular disturbance.

1. I am perfectly calm and relaxed.

4. If the distress is severe, begin tapping before associating into the memory again.

5. The Setup: "Even though I have this _____, I deeply and completely accept myself."

6. The Sequence: **Associate into the memory again and concentrate on being in it, just as if it were happening right now, while carrying out the tapping procedure.** Replay it over and over again -- from the initial shock until you are okay again. If the energy keeps moving around (e.g., the submodalities of the experience shift), keep tapping until it stabilizes. If you do a tapping point and there is no negative energy on it (e.g., nothing happens), then skip that point the next time around on that emotion.

7. **Reduce the emotional charge to a rated one, two or three, for each emotion separately for each memory.** It doesn't all have to be done in one fell swoop. Cycle through the procedure until you have dealt with each of the negative emotions associated with the distressing memory.

The Tapping Points

1. Eyebrow: Where it meets the nose.

2. Beside the eye: About one-half inch back from the orbit.

3. Under the eye: On the top edge, just beneath the eyes, close to the nose.

4. Under the nose: Between the nose and the upper lip.
5. Chin: Half way between the lower lip and the point of the chin.
6. Collarbone: The K27 point, the indentation just under the two bony ridges near the midline of the body, on the right side of the body.
7. Armpit: On the tips of the ribs opposite the nipples (or, for women, about the middle of the bra strap).
8. Thumb: On the outside edge of the thumb, by the base of the nail.
9. Index finger: On the thumb side of the index finger, by the base of the nail.
10. Middle finger: On the thumb side of the middle finger, by the base of the nail.
11. Little finger: On the inside edge of the <u>right</u> little finger, by the base of the nail.
12. Karate Chop: The side of the hand that would perform a karate chop.
13. The Gamet Point (so-called because there are a gamut of things to do while tapping there): The indentation just proximal to the knuckles of the pinky and ring fingers. You can switch hands on this one during the tapping, if necessary.

- tap with the eyes open.
- tap with the eyes closed.
- tap with the eyes looking down to the right (Note: Just the eyes; not the entire head).
- tap with the eyes looking down to the left.
- tap with the eyes circling smoothly clockwise.
- tap with the eyes circling smoothly counter-clockwise.
- tap while humming a tune out loud.
- tap while counting to forty by twos.
- tap while humming a tune out loud.

If the emotion on the memory does not reduce as expected, it means either of two things:

(1) the client keeps slipping into "psychological reversal." In this case, have the client rub the upper left chest about midway between the sternum (breast bone) and the armpit, to suppress the reversal until the procedure can be completed. An alternative is to tap on the Karate Chop point.

(2) the client has switched from focusing on one problem to focusing on another. For example, she may have been working on some phobia and has switched to thinking about how angry she feels about the limitations that her fear has placed on her.

Is this procedure scientifically sound? Well, there is beginning to accumulate a significant body of scientific support. In addition, you can test it out for yourself with relatively little effort.

CHAPTER 11

Sentence Severity: A Practical Measure of Offence Seriousness[14]

ABSTRACT

Scaled values of offence seriousness obtained from the National Survey of Crime Severity in the U.S.A. were used as the dependent measure to determine whether sentence severity (sentence length), as imposed by the Ontario courts on the basis of the Criminal Code of Canada, might serve as an adequate predictor of offence seriousness. A Pearson Product-Moment correlation coefficient of 0.84 was found for a sample of nineteen offenses. Sentence severity appeared to meet the requirements of a useful tool for correctional program evaluation research by a number of criteria such as reliability, validity, meaningfulness, discriminability, accessibility, practicality, and additivity. Some practical problems affecting the measurement of offence seriousness by means of sentence severity were addressed. Tables of ratios of offence seriousness and ratios of sentence severity for pairs of offenses were also presented to assist potential users in choosing the most appropriate scales for their needs.

---

14 by Douglas Quirk, Verna Nutbrown, and Reg Reynolds, Ontario Correctional Institute, Brampton, Ontario.

INTRODUCTION

One of the most basic problems in both jurisprudence and corrections is the need to determine the seriousness of a criminal offence. In jurisprudence, the importance of this determination derives from the need to ensure that sentence is commensurate with the seriousness of the offence. In corrections, this determination is important for two reason: the need to assign priorities to offenders for purposes of correctional programming, and the need to evaluate program effectiveness through observations of graded changes in offenders' post-program behaviours.

Previous attempts to assign degrees of seriousness to various types of offenses have resulted in tools which require often-not-readily-accessible data, which are not easily transferable between jurisdictions, which have frequently been undiscriminating, and which have taken a form unsuitable for use with the most powerful statistical tools in evaluation research. In the present study it is proposed to determine whether sentence severity (as indicated by sentence length) can be used as a measure of offence seriousness. Sentence severity is clearly a discriminating measure, capable of being re-validated across jurisdictions, approximating interval scaling, and readily available for follow-up use in program evaluation research in corrections. Some information is provided on the validation of the proposed measure against the best available published measure of offence seriousness.

HISTORICAL REVIEW

In most outcome evaluation work, treatment effectiveness is determined by the differential recidivism rates for treated and untreated offenders. Typically, recidivism rates are stated as the proportion of recidivists to the total sample of program participants over a follow-up period. Recidivism has most often been expressed as a dichotomous variable established by the presence or absence of specific outcome criteria such as further arrests, further convictions or further incarcerations.

Researchers have long recognized the inadequacies of such all-or-none measures and of the recidivism rates derived from them (Maltz, 1984). The usual criticism is that the dichotomous nature of the recidivism variable ignores a substantial amount of relevant information about the recidivistic event. This reduces the ability of researchers to discriminate among groups and lowers the likelihood of being able to assess varying degrees of impact of correctional programs on individual offender's post-release performances. For example, the post-release changes stemming from correctional programs may take the form of a stepwise series of decrements in both quality and quantity of criminal behaviour. It is possible that each successive intervention may have a cumulative effect, with some interventions affecting the types of crimes committed and others affecting the individual's propensity to commit criminal acts.

A number of attempts have been made to develop methods for the measurement of offence seriousness in order to accommodate this sort of thinking. It has been suggested that improved discrimination might be achieved by examining the distribution of failure times represented by time on the street to recidivism. However, the latter approach measures something equivalent to resistance to recidivism rather than recidivism per se. Thus, while resistance to recidivism is in the form of distributed data, it does not provide a measure of offence seriousness.

Measures of offence seriousness are intended either as tools for evaluating correctional outcomes or else as indices of crime in society. Representative of measures for correctional evaluation are scales where the degree of seriousness is expressed as ordinal weights attached to offence descriptions or offence categories (Gendreau & Leipciger, 1978; Keller & Carlson, 1977; Klein, Newman, Weiss & Bibner, 1983; Moberg & Ericson, 1972; Pease, Ireson, Billingham & Thorpe, 1977; Witherspoon, de Valera & Jenkins, 1973). The best representative of scales developed to measure crime in society is the Offence Seriousness Index (Sellin & Wolfgang, 1964).

The Recidivism Outcome Index (Moberg & Ericson, 1972) is a scale of offence seriousness in which seriousness is evaluated using offender disposition at follow-up. The measures of seriousness range from no recidivism (0) to reimprisonment for felony (10). The Canadian Recidivism Index (Gendreau & Leipciger, 1978) modifies this scale, reducing its eleven categories of disposition to eight. Only the most serious offence is scored, so that its seriousness scores ignore both the quantity of crime and variations in the criminal acts. Since these scales do not provide a continuous base of measurement, they qualify at best as ordinal scales.

The Law Encounter Severity Scale (Witherspoon, et al., 1973) also uses offender disposition as its source of seriousness data. This 39-point scale classifies and ranks follow-up events into five main categories: (a) no law encounter; (b) picked up and released, convicted of misdemeanours; (c) fugitive, absconded or technical violation of parole; (d) convicted and sentenced to less than one year; and (e) convicted and sentenced to more than one year. A dollar figure is affixed to each category to represent the cost of criminal justice processing of the category. The total seriousness score is obtained by multiplying the number of offenses in each category by the cost of that category. Seriousness of offence is thus conceived in terms of society's costs for detection, arrest, detention, trial and imprisonment. This approach points the way to an interesting and economically meaningful measure of seriousness, and provides a continuous base for measurement in dollar costs associated with offenses. As it stands, however, the two sentenced categories are too broad and represent wide variations in cost figures. Discrimination is also limited by failing to take into account the differential nature of the offenses involved.

The Program Rehabilitation Index (Keller & Carlson, 1977) compares the average rated seriousness of the most serious follow-up offence with the average rated seriousness of the most serious original offence. Offenses are classified from 53 offenses identified by their legal labels, and these offenses are rank ordered into 20 categories of seriousness obtained from a study by Gottfredson (1965). Details were not readily available about the scale's development or its psychometric properties. The underlying scale, however, is clearly ordinal in nature, so that the total score for a plurality of recidivistic events cannot properly be obtained by summing seriousness ratings. Moreover, this scale is expressly limited to consideration of the most serious criminal event and thus ignores relevant additional information.

The Offence Seriousness Index developed by Sellin and Wolfgang (1964) adopted a novel approach to the measurement of seriousness, both conceptually and methodologically. Crime seriousness is viewed in terms of the degree of harmful social consequences of components of criminal acts defined in crime descriptions. Eleven scale items were derived: (a) four levels of injury, (b) forcible sex acts, (c) two levels of intimidation, (d) premises forcibly entered, (e) two levels of motor vehicles stolen, and (f) property theft/damage. The total seriousness score is the sum of the seriousness values of each scorable component of the criminal event.

The Offence Seriousness Index has been investigated extensively (Blumstein, 1974; Bridges & Lisagor, 1975; Figlio, 1975; Gottfredson, Young & Laufer, 1980; Hindelang, 1974; Kelly & Winslow, 1973; Lesieur & Lehman, 1975; Rose, 1966; Wagner & Pease, 1978; Walker, 1978; Wellford & Wiatrowski, 1975), replicated internationally (Akman & Normandeau, 1968; Hsu, 1973; Normandeau, 1966; Rossi, Waite, Bose & Berk, 1974; Velez-Diaz & Megargee, 1971) and has gained wide recognition as an index of crime in society. It is probably the most sophisticated method available for measuring offence seriousness. Its use of behaviour descriptions means that, in principle, transferral across jurisdictions should be possible. However, it has some noteworthy limitations for purposes such as program evaluation. Its utility following sentencing is limited because of the difficulty in transforming categories used in legal offence records into the behaviour descriptions employed as scoring criteria. When an offender is undergoing a program to be evaluated, and is directly in contact with researchers, descriptions concerning his current or prior offenses are likely to be too sketchy to permit adequate scoring of pre-program offence seriousness. Also, the offender's own descriptions of offenses frequently do not correspond, even in gross detail, to those records which are available. By the time follow-up is undertaken, the only records available are file records which tend to contain only the category of offence, the number of counts and the sentence imposed. Even if police occurrence reports are available, they rarely contain the kind of detail needed to score offenses on the Offence Seriousness Index. Thus, for most evaluation research, the usefulness and accuracy of this scale in measuring offence seriousness is seriously limited by the quality and quantity of descriptive information available.

In addition to the impracticality of the Offence Seriousness Index for standard use in program evaluation, the scale has another difficulty. Although it, and particularly its next generation development – The National Survey of Crime Severity (Wolfgang, Figlio, Tracy & Singer, 1985) – appear to approximate interval level scaling along which various types of offenses are distributed in a reasonable ordinal sequence, their base data are nominal data derived from different criminal acts or classes of behaviour. This creates some doubt that the scales could really qualify as interval scales to justify the addition of scores across various offence types. The researchers' use of the psychophysical Power Law to establish a subjective scale of seriousness along which offenses might be measured relative to one another creates the impression that a physical scale of equal units underlies the subjective ratio judgements made by their subjects. The nature of this implicit underlying physical scale is conceived as the social harm consequences of various offensive acts. However, this idea really begs the question since it does not provide a physical scale against which to verify ratios in judgements made.

At the same time, Wolfgang, et al. (1985) have provided some information concerning the correspondence of seriousness judgements to a physical scale in incremental dollar loss associated with theft, robbery and arson crimes. At the lower seriousness values, there is some evidence of a fit between the ratios of subjective values and dollar figures (a 1:2:3 ratio expected for dollar amounts of $100, $1,000 and $10,000 or an equivalent series). The subjective weightings for breaking into a school and stealing $10 or $1,000, for example, were 3.08 and 9.72, respectively, roughly in the 1:3 ratio suggested by the psychophysical Power Law. By interpolation, stealing $100 in that setting should receive a weighting of 6.31. Similarly, the values for stealing property worth $100, $1,000 and $10,000 from outside a building were 3.59, 6.86 and 10.94, respectively, approximately in the ratio 1:2:3. However, the seriousness weights for breaking into a home and stealing $100 or $1,000 were 3.14 and 9.60, respectively, varying from the 1:2 ratio which would be predicted. Also, values for arson losses of $10,000, $100,000 and $500,000 received seriousness weights of 12.75, 24.86 and 22.90, respectively. It appears, therefore, as Wolfgang, et al. (1985) mentioned, that there is an attenuation in subjective seriousness values in the upper scale ranges.

The problem of distortion of measures becomes magnified when, assuming interval level scaling, the attempt is made to add Crime Severity weights and to compare summed scores across offence types. According to the National Survey of Crime Severity (NSCS) values, minor injury inflicted in four or five offenses (seriousness score is 7.29 to 8.50), or three perjury, or four false statements, would be equivalent to one murder (seriousness score is 35.71). It seems hard to justify these equivalences. In fact, Sellin and Wolfgang (1964) did not ask their subjects to rate the seriousness of the components of offenses described. Wellford and Wiatrowski (1975), it is true, found a near-perfect correlation (r = .969) between scores obtained from their study sample of ratings of complex events and the sums of ratings of these events' components. Correlation, in this instance however, does not reveal whether the scores obtained were equal or merely in serial concordance with each other. Pease, Ireson and Thorpe (1973) and Wagner and Pease (1978) found that only between 18% and 32% of their respondents actually rated two offenses as twice as serious as one offence. Their results suggest that some people are inclined to under-estimate a multiplicity of offence counts, while others assign incremental importance to a plurality of counts as compared to single or isolated instances of crimes.

It would appear worthwhile, therefore, to examine the additivity of weightings from the National Survey of Crime Severity (NSCS).

Some of the weightings assigned for combined events are almost identical with the sums of the weightings for their components. Murder and robbery combined are weighted at 43.24 and sum from their components to 43.69. Weapons dangerous and robbery yield a combined figure of 9.72 and a summed figure of 10.42. Some other values show considerable variations between their ratings when combined and the sum of ratings for component events. Rape combined with murder is weighted at 52.80, but summed from the components yields a weight of 61.50. Robbery and assault in a single crime is rated at a value of 14.60, but when summed from the components yields a weighting of 19.93. Break, enter and theft is valued at 9.60, but when handled as components sums to 6.81. It seems likely that internal inconsistencies in the scale arise from the absence of a means by which to anchor the subjective ratio scaling in a physically distributed measure.

BASE SCALING

The foremost requirement for an optimally useful and meaningful interval measure of offence seriousness is a continuous physical scale having equal units as the base for comparison. The Law Encounter Severity Scale (Witherspoon et al., 1973) considered the dollar costs of various levels of involvement with the justice system. The NSCS included items scaled for dollar values as well. It is also possible that subjects in the NSCS survey used an implicit scale of values based on dollar amounts for judging criminal events. But dollar values as base scaling are likely to create some difficulties. Temporal and regional variations in economic climate are likely to create error in subjective valuations. For example, a crime associated with a given dollar figure today cannot be compared meaningfully to a crime of a similar dollar value committed ten years ago, unless, of course, adjustments are made to take into account the change in the purchasing power of the dollar over the time period. Exchange rates across international boundaries create additional problems. At the level of the individual, raters from differing socio-economic levels are likely to place differing values on dollar figures. Thus, error of measurement can affect both the base scale itself and judgements made on the base scale.

In seeking a means to measure offence seriousness which is easier and more practical to use in program evaluation than the NSCS scale and which avoids the problems associated with use of dollar values, we examined the kinds of information about offenders and their offenses commonly and relatively easily available to correctional workers. The most likely source of information about offenders' pre-program and post-program offenses available to correctional researchers is the central inmate files maintained by correctional systems. In addition to identification data, inmate files from central record sources are apt to contain little more than: 1) a listing of an offender's offenses and their dates; 2) a record of conviction or non-conviction; 3) the disposition or sentence imposed on each offence; 4) the dates of sentence start and release. Offenses are nominal or categorical data. Offence counts or frequencies are at best ordinal data. Dates of offending or re-offending, along with dates of incarceration and release, provide data distributed on an equal-units physical scale of days (on the street). As suggested earlier, however, this latter information is less concerned with recidivism and offence seriousness than with something akin to resistance to recidivism or to program failure.

Sentence length is also based on a continuous physical scale of days and, in principle, sentence length ought to represent directly the judged seriousness of a criminal event. The advantages of using sentence length as a measure of offence seriousness are many, and include:

1. It uses a reference base continuously distributed in equal units of measurement (days).
2. It is the most readily available and easiest to obtain information about offenses. In most jurisdictions this information is likely to be fairly accurate and easily accessed.

3. It is not capriciously derived. Sentence length is characteristically based upon (a) deliberations about sentence ranges among elected representatives of the community (the government in passing laws), (b) detailed documentation of sentencing precedents, (c) extensive and balanced consideration of the facts of a case during the trial, and (d) judicious consideration of all of the above by the sentencing judge. Theoretically, the sentence length assignment is likely to be subject to minimal error because of the standardization afforded by these considerations. Even pre-trial plea bargaining adds to the value of the outcome by ensuring that offenses which cannot reliably be proved are not completely ignored from sentence computations.

4. It ought to represent offence seriousness meaningfully and in a discriminating way. Not only is there a consistently demonstrated shared agreement among people about the seriousness of various crimes (Figlio, 1975), but also, in simulations, people tend to apply sterner sentences to crimes which are rated as more serious than to crimes rated as less serious (Klein et al., 1983). Moreover, sentence length, along with the type of sentence imposed (prison or probation), meaningfully reflect society's values concerning the seriousness of criminal acts since they necessarily imply a dollar cost figure to be paid by the community in disposing of an offender and his offenses.

Thus, on the face of it, of the readily available types of data on offenders, it appears that sentence length best satisfies the requirements for a measure of offence seriousness, both for evaluation research (ease of access and practical simplicity) and for pure research (quantifiability, meaningfulness and discriminability). It remains to be established whether sentence severity as a measure of offence seriousness satisfies the additional psychometric requirements of reliability, validity, modifiability and generalizability.

METHOD

Measures

The independent measure of sentence severity was based on prison sentences imposed by the courts of Ontario, Canada. These were obtained from the sentencing records of the Ontario Ministry of Correctional Services for offenses defined by the Criminal Code of Canada (CCC) and by federal and provincial acts and statutes. The data available for sentences imposed in Ontario were in the form of numbers of offenders, numbers of counts, mean prison sentence lengths imposed per offence count and range of sentence lengths imposed per offence count. Although these data were available for males and females separately in many offence categories, it was decided not to include data on females. Consequently, ***the independent sentences verity measure is based on male offenders only.*** In order to minimize the effects of possible fluctuations in sentencing practices, due to temporary notoriety for given kinds of offenses afforded by public media attention to particular cases, it was decided to use sentencing data taken across the most recently available three-year interval. Accordingly, sentencing statistics used in this study covered the fiscal years of 1981-82 through 1983-84. The indicator measure chosen to represent sentence severity was the mean sentence length (days in prison) imposed for each offence category. The dependent measure used in this study was based on the National Survey of Crime Severity (Wolfgang et al., 1985), which is the most current, inclusive and psychometrically sophisticated measure of offence seriousness currently available. The NSCS is an update and extension of the original Sellin and Wolfgang (1964) study. The NSCS scale consists of 204 crime descriptions as its stimuli and derives its ratings from the ratio judgements of seriousness made by an extended sample of 60,000 Americans residing in the United States. Its reference, therefore is to a national U.S. jurisdiction.

Procedure

The first step was to obtain a set of offenses on which to measure the dependent and independent variables. The list of 204 NSCS crime descriptions was examined, and those which would not result in a prison sentence in this jurisdiction were excluded. This was necessary because the data available on sentencing were concerned solely with prison sentences and not other terms of penalty such as fines, probation, etc. The next step was to go through the list of NSCS crime descriptions again and fit each with the most appropriate offence category label from the Criminal Code of Canada (CCC). The resulting set of offenses and their crime descriptions were then submitted (a) to a psychologist expert in inmate classifications for an exercise of judgement on the validity of the offence/crime description matches and (b) to a group of six forensic psychologists for the identification of offenses for which the relationship between sentence severity and offence seriousness might be partially obscured due to varying perceptions of offence seriousness in the U.S.A. and Canada. There was strong agreement that drug offenses are likely jurisdictional variants (interjudge reliability coefficient of .80). In addition, on the basis of the differences between the two countries in gun control laws, weapons offenses were designated as jurisdictional variants. The next step was to generate the sentence severity and NSCS offence seriousness data associated with the list of offenses. The sentence severity measure posed little difficulty. Sentence severity (mean sentence length) was calculated for all offenses for which 24 or more counts of the offence were available and at least one count of the offence occurred during each of the three years of the observation period. For the NSCS offence seriousness data, however, the task was not quite so straight-forward since many of the offence categories were associated with a multiplicity of crime descriptions. The solution to the problem of choosing the value for NSCS offence seriousness to attach to each offence category was to conduct two separate studies of the relationship between sentence severity and offence seriousness.

The purpose of both studies was to determine the validity of sentence severity as a measure of offence seriousness. In each study, validity is demonstrated by a high correlation between sentence severity and the criterion measure of offence seriousness obtained from the NSCS seriousness scores.

Study 1. Ideally, the choice of values for the seriousness of each offence should be guided by the goal of reducing measurement error. Measurement error was reduced in Study 1: (a) by eliminating the identified jurisdictional variants and (b) by averaging the NSCS offence seriousness scores for the range of crime descriptions within any single CCC category. The value used as the measure of offence seriousness for each offence category, then, was the mean NSCS offence seriousness value for crime descriptions in that category. This approach assumes that the range of crime descriptions used in the NSCS was representative of the range of criminal acts which typically occur in any given offence category and that the mean sentence length calculated for the sentence severity measure was based on a similar range of criminal acts. Table 1 contains the 19 offenses analyzed in Study 1.

Study 1 Offences and Associated Scale Values for Sentence Severity and Offence Seriousness*

CCC offence title	Sentence severity	Offence seriousness	Number of crime descriptions
1. Murder (one and two)	7555.9	40.33	7
2. Attempted murder	2218.4	28.84	1
3. Rape	1553.3	25.32	3
4. Attempted rape	947.9	16.86	1
5. Kidnap	756.0	22.83	2
6. Robbery	605.8	19.86	15
7. Criminal negligence causing death	595.8	19.48`	1
8. Arson	426.2	19.97	3
9. Accessory after the fact	301.5	7.22	1
10. Extortion	293.8	10.27	1
11. Aggravated assault	265.5	14.35	12

12. Break and enter	196.3	8.65	5
13. Fraud	159.0	9.29	8
14. Perjury	151.1	11.37	1
15. Living off avails	131.3	6.12	1
16. Bribery	128.4	12.89	2
17. Theft over	126.5	9.80	7
18. Assault causing bodily harm	111.2	11.42	9
19. Take vehicle without consent	44.1	4.45	1

Study 2. In Study 2 the robustness of the relationship between sentence severity and offence seriousness was examined under conditions presumed to increase measurement error. In this study, the range of offenses was extended, the jurisdictional variants were included rather than excluded, and the value of offence seriousness was determined by choosing the single most representative crime description associated with each offence category. The latter task was accomplished by submitting the list of crime descriptions to the previously-mentioned expert in inmate classification for a decision on the most representative or modal example of each offence category. The 33 offenses analyzed in Study 2 are presented in Table 2.

Table 2 Offence categories and their selected most representative Crime Descriptions and their Offence Seriousness values.

CCC offence title	NSCS crime description	Sentence severity	Offence seriousness	Number of crime descriptions
1. Murder (one and two)	A person stabs a victim to death.	7555.9	35.71	7
2. Attempted murder	A person stabs a victim with a knife. The victim requires hospitalization.	2218.4	18.02	1
3. Rape	A man forcibly rapes a woman. No other physical injury occurs.	1553.3	25.85	3

4. Attempted rape	A man drags a woman into an alley, tears her clothes, but flees before she is physically or sexually attacked.	947.9	16.86	1
5. Kidnap	A person kidnaps a victim.	756.0		2
6. Robbery	A person, using force, robs a victim of $1,000. No physical harm.	605.8	21.18	15
7. Criminal negligence causing death	A person kills a victim by recklessly driving an automobile.	595.8	19.48	1
8. Arson	A person intentionally sets a fire to a building causing $100,00 of damage.	426.2	24.86	3
9. Attempted robbery	A person attempts to rob a victim but runs away when a police car approaches.	343.7	3.26	
10. Accessory after the fact	A person willingly hides out a bank robber.	301.5	7.22	1
11. Extortion	A person threatens to harm a victim unless the victim gives him money. The victim gives him $1,000 and is not harmed.	293.8	10.27	

12. Indecent assault	A man runs his hands over the body of a female victim, then runs away.	265.5	5.12	12
13. Aggravated assault	A man beats his wife with his fists. She requires hospitalization.	265.5	18.3	
14. Break and enter	A person breaks into a building and steals property worth $10.	196.3	3.22	5
15, Attempted break and enter	A person attempts to break into a home but runs away when a police car approaches.	192.9	4.22	
16. Traffic in narcotics	A person sells heroin to others	168.0	20.65	
17. Fraud	A person illegally gets monthly welfare cheques of $200.	159.0	8.27	8
18. Weapons dangerous	A person knowingly carries an illegal knife.	152.5	2.44	
19. Perjury	A person knowingly lies under oath during a trial.	151.1	11.37	1
20. Possession of stolen property	A person knowingly buys stolen property from the person who stole it.	131.5	5.00	
21. Living off avails	A person runs a prostitution racket.	131.3	6.12	1

22. Bribery	A company pays a bribe of $10,000 to a legislator to vote for a law favouring the company.	128.4	14.48	2
23. Possession of a restricted drug	A person has some marijuana for his own use.	127.2	1.34	
24. Theft over	A person steals $1,000 worth of merchandise from the counter of a department store.	126.5	7.63	
25. Threatening	A person threatens to seriously injure a victim.	121.3	9.29	
26. Assault causing bodily harm	A person intentionally injures a victim. The victim is treated by a doctor and hospitalized.	111.2	11.95	9
27. Possession of a narcotic	A person has some heroin for his own use.	47.7	5.42	
28. Theft under	A person steals property worth $100 from outside a building.	47.6	3.59	
29. Take vehicle without consent	A person steals an unlocked vehicle and later abandons it undamaged.	44.1	4.45	1

30. Simple assault	A person beats a 42.1 7.29 victim with his fists. The victim is hurt but does not require medical treatment	42.1	7.29	
31. False statement	A person knowingly makes false entries on a document that the court has requested for a criminal trial.	34.4	9.17	
32. Fail to appear	A person, free on bail for committing a serious crime, purposefully fails to appear in court on the day of his trial.	22.3	6.30	
33. Petty trespass	A person trespasses in the backyard of a private home.	6.3	0.64	

Two adjustments of the data were considered. Firstly, it had been determined by the psychologist expert in inmate classifications that the NSCS offence categories for murder one and murder two were not differentiated in the NSCS crime descriptions in ways meaningful to the CCC murder categories. For present purposes, therefore, murder one and murder two were combined, the sentence lengths for murder were averaged, and NSCS crime descriptions were found to represent the combined murder category. Secondly, given the range of social harm consequences deliberately built into the NSCS crime descriptions, it might have been justifiable to eliminate crime descriptions with extreme values on the grounds that they might have distorted the representativeness of the derived (averaged) seriousness scores. However, the mean and median values for the seriousness of each offence category were approximately equal, suggesting that no significant distortion due to outliers had occurred. Therefore, no crime descriptions were eliminated from the present dataset on this basis.

RESULTS

Study 1

As Table 1 illustrates, the set of offenses in the dataset are discriminable not only by the descriptive characteristics suggested by their legal labels, but also by the degrees of two metric characteristics, namely sentence length and (judged) offence seriousness. The ordinal progression of offence seriousness values shows a good correspondence to the rank order of the mean sentence severity scores, albeit with some mismatches. This apparent concordance is expressed in a Pearson correlation of .84 obtained between these two sets of scores.

Next, the two scales were plotted on linear co-ordinate paper, and it was observed that the rate of change in the upper ranges was greater for sentence severity than for offence seriousness. Thus, it seemed clear that the two variables did not follow a parallel linear path with respect to one another. This fact suggested the appropriateness of transforming scores to improve linearity. Unfortunately, for want of a criterion on which to scale the real intervals between offence categories, it was not possible to determine which of the two variables to transform or which type of transformation might be expected to make appropriate corrections to either variable. From the point of view of offence seriousness, sentence severity accelerates in the upper ranges; and from the point of view of sentence severity, offence seriousness is truncated in the upper ranges. Moreover, to apply a transformation to the sentence severity measure would add another minor complexity to the task of the correctional evaluation researcher working with sentence severity as a measure of seriousness. These two considerations seemed sufficient to warrant trying transformations on both of the variables.

Table 3 presents the results of the regressions of untransformed offence seriousness on variously transformed sentence severity, and of untransformed sentence severity on variously transformed offence seriousness. It is worth noting that, although some transformations do improve the correlation between the two scales, particularly the logarithmic (r=.93), square root (r=.92) and quadratic (r=.91) transformations of sentence severity and the quadratic (r=.99), exponential (r=.93), and power (r=.89) transformations of offence seriousness -- it is almost unnecessary to transform the data since the basic relationship between the two variables (r=.84) appears reasonably robust even in untransformed form.

Table 3

Regressions of Raw Offence Seriousness on Variously Transformed Sentence Severity and of Raw Sentence Severity on Variously Transformed Offence Seriousness (Study 1 Offences).

Transformation model	Transformation equation	X = sentence severity Y = offence seriousness	X = offence seriousness Y = sentence severity
Untransformed	Y=A+BX	0.837	0.837
Inverted	Y=A+B/X	0.648	0.458
Reciprocal	1/Y=A+B/X	0.849	0.849
Square Root	Y=A+B/X	0.922	0.755
Exponential	$Y=Ae^{BX}$	0.656	0.927
Power	$Y=AX^B$	0.889	0.889
Logarithmic	Y=A+BLnX	0.927	0.656
Quadratic	$Y+A+BX+CX^2$	0.911	0.985

Study 2

As Table 2 illustrates, the concordance between sentence severity and offence seriousness remains apparent, even with the extended range of offenses, the identified jurisdictional variants, and the single offence seriousness values to represent each offence category (r = .68). The same divergence in the upper scale ranges that was found in Study 1 continues in Study 2. However, when these data were plotted on linear co-ordinate paper there was considerably greater variability between the two scales than had been noted in the Study 1 data.

As in Study 1, it was decided to determine the effects of various types of transformations of each of the variables on the correlation between the two variables. Table 4 presents the regression of each scale in raw form on the other in variously transformed form. It will be seen from Table 4 that the quadratic transformation again improves the correlation although the reciprocal and square root transformations (perhaps by restricting variability) produced an even higher set of correlations. As expected, the correlation coefficients derived from transformed scores were slightly lower than those found in Study 1.

Table 4. Regressions of Raw Sentence Severity on Variously Transformed

Transformation model	Transformation equation	R (with jurisdictional variants)	R (without jurisdictional variants)
Untransformed	$Y=A+BX$	0.678	0.714
Inverted	$Y=A+B/X$	0.346	0.374
Reciprocal	$1/Y=A+B/X$	0.837	0.927
Square Root	$Y=A+B/X$	0.762	0.794
Exponential	$Y=Ae^{BX}$	0.447	0.480
Power	$Y=AX^B$	0.663	0.728
Logarithmic	$Y=A+BLnX$	0.721	0.748
Quadratic	$Y+A+BX+CX^2$	0.748	0.781

DISCUSSION

Study 1 suggests that sentence severity is both a valid and a reliable measure of offence seriousness. A correlation coefficient can indicate two things: (a) the degree of functional relationship between two variables, or the extent to which one variable predicts the other variable (validity); and, by squaring its value, (b) the accuracy of the prediction (reliability). The high correlation obtained (r=.84) represents high predictive validity attenuated partly by sampling bias and partly by measurement bias – the two sets of variables were selected to match each other on a face valid basis by one expert, and the data were drawn from two different jurisdictions (U.S.A. and Canada). Given these two sources of error in the data, the observed degree of concomitance between the two scales is quite good. The hypothesis of a valid relationship between sentence severity and offence seriousness is supported, and each of the measures is a relatively reliable predictor of the other.

Study 2 demonstrated that the strong mutual relationship between sentence severity and offence seriousness is only moderately attenuated (r=.68) by the methodological changes in the construction of the scale of measurements, i.e., the extended range of offenses, the inclusion of offenses regarded as jurisdictional variants, and the use of the single most representative crime description in determining offence seriousness. However, the lower correlation obtained in Study 2 suggests that jurisdictional differences in judgments of the seriousness of particular offenses (in combination with other factors) may contribute error to the measurement of seriousness. Two corollaries would follow. Firstly, judges in a local jurisdiction probably better reflect the local community's concepts of seriousness than judges from other jurisdictions, and local estimates of offence seriousness based on the sentencing practices of local judges should be obtained whenever possible. Secondly, a replication of the present study in each jurisdiction is advisable before assuming that offence seriousness estimates obtained from other jurisdictions, e.g., NSCS estimates, would in all cases correspond closely to estimates obtained from data collected locally.

Comparison of Sentence Severity and Offence Seriousness

It might appropriately be said that, in seeking to find a measure of offence seriousness which is convenient to use, the present study has merely "re-invented the scales of justice". Perhaps a convenient to use, simple, and valid psychometric scale of offence seriousness, in the form of sentence length, has been available all along to workers in correctional program evaluation. We contend that the sentences imposed by judges amount to an application of the same method of psychophysical judgment used

in the most popular and sophisticated method for scaling offence seriousness which is currently available (Wolfgang, et al., 1985). Indeed, in many ways, using sentences imposed by court judges has methodological advantages over the procedure of asking samples of lay raters to perform judgments equivalent to those made by court judges. These advantages include the possibility that raters, as compared to court judges, may undertake their ratings more capriciously, and may not be as familiar with the range and characteristics of criminal acts. Moreover, court judges have access to all of the standardizing and correcting means available in the justice system. Finally, unlike the raters in the NSCS study who were required to make psychophysical judgements in psychological space anchored only by a standard modulus, court judges have the advantage of having a socially and economically meaningful physical scale divided into equal units (days) along which to distribute their judgements of offence seriousness.

Of course, such arguments about the relative merits of one scale over another, although possibly pointing to salient features of each scale, are apt to be specious. In the last analysis, the judgement about the relative merits of two measures of the same thing will be made by the user. It would seem appropriate, therefore, to provide the potential user of a scale of offence seriousness with the basic data on which he or she can exercise appropriate judgement.

In order to permit meaningful addition of values for various kinds of offenses, a scale of offence seriousness must be at least at the interval level of scaling. If a scale is distributed in equal units of measurement, it should be possible to identify the orderly arithmetic progression of the various elements, and the equivalence of proportions among pairs of elements across the range of the scale. These requirements form the essential basis for

Stevens' (1957) Power Law was the basis on which Sellin and Wolfgang (1964) and Wolfgang, et al. (1985) determined their offence seriousness values. Actually, the Power Law requires that a physical scale form part of the equation. It will be recalled that, for want of an actual physical scale of offence seriousness, Sellin and Wolfgang (1964) created a conceptual physical scale in referring to the social harm consequences of crime. In evaluating the ratios between offence types, therefore, this implicit "physical" scale needs to be kept in mind, as well as the idea that one aspect of the social harm consequences of an offence may be represented by the duration of the protection of society required, i.e., the length of the sentence imposed.

The Power Law (Stevens, 1957) states that equal physical ratios are psychologically equal. That is, if ratios were to be constructed between scale values representing pairs of offence categories, an adjudicator should be able to determine, as a subjective judgement, the sets of ratios which best represent the social harm consequences of given types of acts.

Tables 5 and 6 present the ratios, derived from the NSCS offence seriousness and the sentence severity scales, respectively, between pairs of CCC offence categories. In these tables, in order to employ "real" NSCS values for offence seriousness, the longer list of 33 pairings used in Study 2 is employed, with offence seriousness values based on the single most representative crime description for each offence category. The codes used to represent each offence category refer to the list of offenses and crime descriptions in the order shown in Table 2. In Tables 5 and 6, the ratios have been rounded to the nearest whole number for ease of reading.[15]

---

15   Note: Offence codes are 1. Murder; 2. Attempt 15murder; 3. Rape; 4. Attempt rape; 5. Kidnap; 6. Robbery; 7. Criminal negligence causing death; 8. Arson; 9. Attempted robbery; 10. Accessory after fact; 11. Extortion; 12. Indecent assault; 13. Aggravated assault; 14. Break and enter; 15. Attempted break and enter; 16. Traffic in narcotics; 17. Fraud; 18. Weapons dangerous; 19. Perjury; 20. Possession stolen property; 21. Living off avails; 22. Bribery; 23. Possession of a restricted drug; 24. Theft over; 25. Threatening; 26. Assault causing bodily harm; 27. Possession of a narcotic; 28. Theft under; 29; Take vehicle without consent; 30. Simple assault; 31. False statement; 32. Fail to Appear.

Table 5. Ratios Among Offences According to NSCS Seriousness Values (Study 2 Offences)

Offence code	1	2	3	4	5	6	7	8	9	10	11	12	13	14	15	16	17	18	19	20	21	22	23	24	25	26	27	28	29	30	31	32
1	-																															
2	2	-																														
3	1	1	-																													
4	2	1	2	-																												
5	2	1	1	1	-																											
6	5	2	3	2	3	-																										
7	2	1	1	1	1	1	-																									
8	1	1	1	1	1	1	1	-																								
9	11	6	8	5	7	2	6	8	-																							
10	5	3	4	2	3	1	3	3	1	-																						
11	4	2	3	2	2	1	2	2	1	1	-																					
12	7	4	5	3	4	2	4	5	1	1	1	-																				
13	2	1	1	1	2	1	1	1	1	1	1	1	-																			
14	11	6	8	5	7	3	6	8	1	2	3	2	6	-																		
15	9	4	6	4	5	2	5	6	1	2	2	1	4	1	-																	
16	2	1	1	1	1	1	1	1	1	1	1	1	1	1	1	-																
17	4	2	3	2	3	1	2	3	1	3	4	2	8	1	1	2	-															
18	15	7	11	7	9	3	7	10	1	1	1	1	2	1	1	9	3	-														
19	3	2	2	2	2	1	2	2	1	1	1	1	2	1	2	2	1	1	-													
20	7	4	5	3	4	2	4	5	1	1	2	1	4	1	1	4	2	1	1	-												
21	6	3	4	3	4	1	3	4	1	1	2	1	3	1	1	3	1	1	2	1	-											
22	3	3	2	3	2	1	2	4	1	1	1	1	3	1	1	3	1	1	1	1	1	-										
23	27	13	19	13	16	6	15	19	2	5	8	4	14	2	3	15	6	2	9	4	5	11	-									

Table 6. Ratios Among Offences According to Sentence Severity Values (Study 2 Offences)

Offence code	1	2	3	4	5	6	7	8	9	10	11	12	13	14	15	16	17	18	19	20	21	22	23	24	25	26	27	28	29	30	31	32
1	-																															
2	3	-																														
3	5	1	-																													
4	8	2	2	-																												
5	10	3	2	1	-																											
6	13	4	3	2	1	-																										
7	13	4	3	2	1	1	-																									
8	18	5	4	2	2	1	1	-																								
9	22	7	5	3	2	2	2	1	-																							
10	25	7	5	3	3	2	2	1	1	-																						
11	26	8	5	3	3	2	2	2	1	1	-																					
12	26	8	5	3	3	2	2	2	1	1	1	-																				
13	29	8	6	4	3	2	2	2	1	1	1	1	-																			
24	5	2	3	2	3	1	3	3	1	2	1	2	1	1	3	1	1	2	1	1	2	1	-									
25	4	2	3	2	2	1	2	3	1	1	1	2	1	1	2	1	1	1	1	1	2	1	1	-								
26	3	2	2	1	2	1	2	2	1	1	1	2	1	1	2	1	1	1	1	1	1	1	1	1	-							
27	7	3	5	3	4	2	4	5	1	2	2	3	1	1	4	2	1	2	1	2	3	1	1	1	2	-						
28	10	5	7	5	6	2	5	7	2	3	3	5	1	1	6	2	1	3	2	2	4	2	2	2	3	2	-					
29	8	4	6	4	5	2	4	6	2	2	2	4	1	1	5	2	1	3	1	1	3	1	2	2	3	2	1	-				
30	5	3	4	2	3	1	3	3	1	1	1	3	1	1	3	1	1	2	1	1	2	1	1	1	2	1	1	1	1	-		
31	4	2	3	2	2	1	2	3	1	1	1	2	1	1	2	1	1	1	1	1	2	1	1	1	1	1	1	1	1	1	-	
32	6	3	4	1	3	1	3	4	1	2	1	3	1	1	3	1	1	1	1	1	2	1	1	1	2	2	1	1	1	1	2	-

																		–
																	–	2
																–	1	2
															–	1	1	2
														–	1	1	1	2
													–	1	1	1	1	2
												–	2	2	3	3	3	5
											–	1	3	3	3	3	4	5
										–	1	1	3	3	3	3	4	6
									–	1	1	1	3	3	3	3	4	6
								–	1	1	1	1	3	3	3	3	4	6
							–	1	1	1	1	1	3	3	3	3	4	6
						–	1	1	1	1	1	1	3	3	3	3	4	6
					–	1	1	1	1	1	1	1	3	3	3	4	4	7
				–	1	1	1	1	1	1	1	1	3	3	4	4	4	7
			–	1	1	1	1	1	1	1	1	1	3	3	4	4	5	7
		–	1	1	1	1	1	1	1	1	1	2	4	4	4	4	5	8
	–	1	1	1	1	2	2	2	2	2	2	2	4	4	5	5	6	9
–	1	1	1	1	1	2	2	2	2	2	2	2	4	4	5	5	6	9
1	1	2	2	2	2	2	2	2	2	2	2	2	6	6	6	6	8	12
2	2	2	2	2	2	2	2	2	2	2	2	3	6	6	7	7	8	13
2	2	2	2	2	2	2	2	2	2	2	3	3	6	6	7	7	9	13
2	2	2	2	2	2	2	2	2	2	2	3	3	6	6	7	7	9	14
2	2	2	2	2	2	3	3	3	3	3	3	3	7	7	8	8	10	15
2	2	3	3	3	3	3	3	3	3	3	4	4	9	9	10	10	12	19
3	3	4	4	4	4	5	5	5	5	5	5	5	13	13	14	14	17	27
3	3	4	4	5	5	5	5	5	5	5	5	5	13	13	14	14	18	27
4	4	5	5	5	5	6	6	6	6	6	6	7	16	16	17	18	22	
5	5	6	6	6	6	7	7	7	8	8	8	9	20	20	22	23	28	43
8	8	9	10	10	10	12	12	12	12	12	13	14	33	33	35	37	45	70
11	12	13	14	15	15	17	17	17	17	18	18	20	47	47	50	53	65	100
39	39	45	48	50	50	58	58	59	59	60	62	68	158	160	171	179	220	339
14	15	16	17	18	19	20	21	22	23	24	25	26	27	28	29	30	31	32

Examples may facilitate the reading of these tables. Table 5 shows that, according to the NSCS offence seriousness scale, approximately 5 minor assaults (Offence code 30) would be equivalent to one murder (Offence code 1), whereas Table 6 shows that, according to the sentence severity scale, it would take 179 minor assaults to be equivalent of one murder. Similarly, according to the NSCS offence seriousness scale, one theft-over is equivalent to one robbery, whereas, according to the sentence severity scale, five theft-overs (Offence code 24) would be equivalent to one robbery (Offence code 6).

Sentence Severity Application

A final note needs to be made concerning the application of sentence severity as a measure of offence seriousness. In the present study, sentence severity has taken into account prison sentences only. Another type of sentence, namely Probation, has not yet been considered. Since probation is also a sentence for offenses, it should be included in some way in any comprehensive sentence severity scale of offence seriousness.

It seems clear that probation, although also a sentence, is construed as less severe than a sentence to prison. In searching for a reasonable basis on which to add probation terms to prison sentences in computing sentence severity, the present writers considered the relative societal costs involved in the two kinds of sentences. It was found that in this jurisdiction (Ontario), at the time when these data were being considered, the costs of incarcerating an offender were about 31 times greater than the cost of probation supervision. This, of course, is a very convenient figure. Apparently, in this jurisdiction, one month of probation is equivalent to one day of prison, as a measure of the judged social harm consequences of offenses as that is reflected in the cost which society is willing to bear in disposing of offenses. Moreover, again conveniently, in this jurisdiction, prison terms are imposed and reported in days of sentence, and probation terms are imposed and reported in months of sentence. It would seem appropriate in applications of the sentence severity scale to add to the total prison days, the number of months of probation sentences imposed.

SUMMARY

Sentence severity, as indicated by length of sentence, was proposed as a readily available and practical measure of offence seriousness. Sentence severity was compared with the best available method of measuring offence seriousness and was found to be both a valid and a reliable measure of offence seriousness. Some practical and research considerations affecting the use of various measures of offence seriousness were discussed. Ratio comparisons between pairs of NSCS offence seriousness and sentence severity measures were presented to assist users in deciding for themselves which measure might best suit their needs. It was concluded that sentence severity appeared to conform to most of the requirements for a psychometric scale, including validity, reliability, discriminability and meaningfulness, while also providing an adequate approximation to quantifiability for purposes of additivity. It remains to be determined whether sentence severity is generalizable beyond this jurisdiction.

REFERENCES

Akman, D.D., & Normandeau, A. (1968). Towards the measurement of criminality in Canada: A replication study. Acta Criminologica 1, 135-260.

Blumstein, A. (1974). Seriousness weights in an index of crime. American Sociological Review, 39, (6), 854-864.

Bridges, G.S., & Lisagor, N.S. (1975). Scaling seriousness: An evaluation of magnitude and category scaling techniques. The Journal of Criminology, 66, (2), 215-221.

Carroll, J.S., & Payne, J.W. (1977). Crime seriousness, recidivism risk, and causal attribution in judgements of prison term by students and experts. Journal of Applied Psychology, 62, 595-602.

Figlio, R.M. (1975). The seriousness of offenses: An evaluation by offenders and nonoffenders. Journal of Criminal Law, Criminology, and Police Science, 66, 189-200.

Gendreau, P., & Leipciger, M. (1978). The development of a recidivism measure and its application in Ontario. Canadian Journal of Criminology, 20, 3-17.

Gottfredson, D.M. (1965). A strategy for the study of correctional effectiveness. Paper presented at the 4th session of the International Criminological Congress, Montreal, Canada.

Gottfredson, S., Young, K.L., & Laufer, W.S. (1980). Additivity and interactions in offence seriousness scales. Journal of Research in Crime and Delinquency, (Jan.), 26-41.

Hindelang, M.J. (1974). The Uniform Crime Reports revisited. Journal of Criminal Justice, 2, 1-7.

Hsu, M. (1973). Cultural and sexual differences in the judgement of criminal offenses. Journal of Criminal Law, Criminology, and Police Science, 64, 348-353.

Kellar, S.L., & Carlson, K.A. (1977). Development of an index to evaluate programs in a correctional setting. Canadian Journal of Criminology and Corrections, 19, 263-277.

Kelly, D.H., & Winslow, R.W. (1973). Seriousness of delinquent behaviour: An alternative perspective. Journal of Criminal Law and Criminology, 64, (3), 124-135.

Klein, R.J., Newman, I., Weiss, D.M., & Bibner, R.F. (1983). The Continuum of Criminal Offenses instrument: Further development and modification of Sellin and Wolfgang's original index. Journal of Offender Counselling, Services and Rehabilitation, 1, 33-53.

Lesieur, H.R., & Lehman, P.M. (1975). Remeasuring delinquency: A replication and critique. British Journal of Criminology, 15, 69-80.

Maltz, M.D. (1984). Recidivism. New York, N.Y.: Academic Press.

Moberg, D.O., & Ericson, R.C. (1972). A New Recidivism Outcome Index. Federal Probation, 36, 50-57.

Normandeau, A. (1966). The measurement of delinquency in Montreal. Journal of Criminal Law, Criminology, and Police Science, 57, 172-177.

Pease, K., Ireson, J., Billingham, S., & Thorpe, J. (1977). The development of a scale of offence seriousness. International Journal of Criminology and Penology, 5, 17-29.

Pease, K., Ireson, J., & Thorpe, J. (1974). Additivity assumption in the measurement of delinquency. British Journal of Criminology, 14, 256-263.

Rose, G.N.G. (1966). Concerning the measurement of delinquency. British Journal of Criminology, 6, 414-421.

Rossi, P.N., Waite, C., Bose, C.E., & Berk, R.E. (1974) The seriousness of crimes: Normative structure and individual differences. American Sociological Review, 39, 224-237.

Sellin, T., & Wolfgang, M.F. (1964). The Measurement of Delinquency, New York, N.Y.: Wiley.

Stevens, S.S. (1957). On the psychophysical law. Psychological Review, 64, 153-181.

Velez-Diaz, A., & Megargee, E.I. (1971). An investigation of differences in value judgements between youthful offenders and nonoffenders in Puerto Rico. Journal of Criminal Law, Criminology, and Police Science, 61, 549-553.

Wagner, H., & Pease, K. (1978). On adding up scores of offence seriousness. British Journal of Criminology, 18, (1), 175-178.

Walker, M.A. (1978). Measuring the seriousness of crime, British Journal of Criminology, 18. (4), 348-364.

Wellford, C.F., & Wiatrowski, M. (1975). On the measurement of delinquency. The Journal of Criminal Law and Criminology, 66, (2), 175-188.

Witherspoon, A.D., de Valera, E.K., & Jenkins, W.B. (1973). The Law Encounter Severity Scale (LESS): A criterion of criminal behaviour and recidivism. Montgomery, AL.: Rehabilitation Research Foundation.

Wolfgang, M.F., Figlio, R.M., Tracy, P.E., & Singer, S.I. (1985). The National Survey of Crime Severity. U.S. Department of Justice.

CHAPTER 12

Dualism As It Relates To Unity With God

Perhaps you are familiar with the well known injunction to "seek ye diligently and teach one another words of wisdom; yea, seek ye out of the best books words of wisdom; seek learning even by study, and also by faith." (Part of a revelation given to Joseph Smith in 1832 and recorded in Section 86 of the Community of Christ's book of Doctrine and Covenants):

[Sec 85:36a] ... verily I say unto you, my friends, Call your solemn assembly, as I have commanded you; and as all have not faith, seek ye diligently and teach one another words of wisdom; yea, seek ye out of the best books words of wisdom; seek learning even by study, and also by faith.

Now, I don't know what you think about the Book of Mormon, but I consider it to contain some really inspired writing. It may be that it is not the history that it purports to be, or it may be that it is. Perhaps Joseph Smith was inspired to present his understanding of God in the context of a fictional history in the same way that it now appears many of the writers of biblical scriptures did – the story of Job, for example – or perhaps the events it portrays happened just the way the Book of Mormon says they did. But whether or not these sacred stories were *intended* to be transformative rather than historical, in the same way that the sacred stories of the Eastern religions were intended to be transformative rather than historical, it really doesn't matter very much to me. For me, the Book of Mormon is one of those "best books" from which to seek words of wisdom, and in my opinion, and it has plenty of those. Consider, for example, the following passage from the first chapter of 2 Nephi, where Nephi's father, Lehi, says to his eldest son, Jacob,

"... for there must be an opposition in all things. If not so, my first born in the wilderness, righteousness could not be brought to pass; neither wickedness; neither holiness nor misery; neither good nor bad. Wherefore, all things must be a compound in one. Wherefore, if it should be one body, it must remain as dead, having no life, neither death nor corruption, nor incorruption, happiness nor misery, neither sense nor insensibility. Wherefore, it must have been created for a thing of naught; wherefore, there would have been no purpose in the end of its creation."

And a few verses later, it says:

"...Now, behold, if Adam had not transgressed, he would not have fallen; but he would have remained in the garden of Eden. And all things which were created must have remained in the same state which they were, after they were created; and they must have remained forever, and had no end. They would have had no children; wherefore, they would have remained in a state of innocence, having no joy, for they knew no misery; doing no good, for they knew no sin. But, behold, all things have been done in the wisdom of him who knows all things. Adam fell, that men might be; and men are, that they might have joy."

Throughout the centuries, the more mystical followers of both Eastern and Western religious traditions have sought to heal their separation from God through a variety of practices designed to allow them to transcend the duality referred to in the Book of Mormon, and return to unity with God. Carolyn Brock, in an article written for the Herald, reminds us that the images portrayed by the Sufi mystics "invite us to give up the grief of our separation and be drawn into intimate companionship with an exuberant God who delights in us."

What shall we do with such foreign ideas? Well, the Book of Mormon might suggest that we might at least consider them, for in 2 Nephi we also read:

[2 Ne 12:53] Thou fool, that shall say, A bible, we have got a bible, and we need no more bible.

[2 Ne 12:54] Have ye obtained a bible save it were by the Jews?

[2 Ne 12:55] Know ye not that there are more nations than one?

[2 Ne 12:56] Know ye not that I, the Lord your God, have created all men, and that I remember those who are upon the isles of the sea; and that I rule in the heavens above, and in the earth beneath;

[2 Ne 12:57] And I bring forth my word unto the children of men, yea, even upon all the nations of the earth?

[2 Ne 12:58] Wherefore murmur ye, because that ye shall receive more of my word?

[2 Ne 12:59] Know ye not that the testimony of two nations is a witness unto you that I am God, that I remember one nation like unto another?

[2 Ne 12:60] Wherefore, I speak the same words unto one nation like unto another.

[2 Ne 12:61] And when the two nations shall run together, the testimony of the two nations shall run together also.

[2 Ne 12:62] And I do this that I may prove unto many, that I am the same yesterday, to-day, and for ever; and that I speak forth my words according to mine own pleasure.

[2 Ne 12:63] And because that I have spoken one word, ye need not suppose that I can not speak another; for my work is not yet finished; neither shall it be, until the end of man; neither from that time hence forth and for ever.

[2 Ne 12:64] Wherefore, because that ye have a bible, ye need not suppose that it contains all my words; neither need ye suppose that I have not caused more to be written:

[2 Ne 12:65] For I command all men, both in the east, and in the west, and in the north, and in the south, and in the islands of the sea, that they shall write the words which I speak unto them:

[2 Ne 12:66] For out of the books which shall be written, I will judge the world, every man according to his works, according to that which is written.

[2 Ne 12:67] For behold, I shall speak unto the Jews, and they shall write it:

[2 Ne 12:68] And I shall also speak unto the Nephites, and they shall write it;

[2 Ne 12:69] And I shall also speak unto the other tribes of the house of Israel, which I have led away, and they shall write it;

[2 Ne 12:70] And I shall also speak unto all nations of the earth, and they shall write it.

And the implication of all this is that we might at least consider whether wisdom is to found in these other "good books" as it is to be found in our own scriptures.

Carolyn Brock seems to suggest that the Christian mystics central quest was "union with the Divine" which, in my convoluted, ecumenical way of thinking, brings us to Buddhism. In Buddhism, the attempt to attain unity with ultimate reality – Christians would call that the great "I am" – has typically involved extended periods of meditation in which the meditator tries to learn to quiet his or her mind to the point of becoming aware of reality unconstructed, as it were, by thought (or, if you like, reality uninfluenced by expectations). In that moment, known as "enlightenment," the opposition referred to above – the duality by which the universe is organized into what is and what is not – is extinguished, and the meditator returns to a unity with ultimate reality. To think of that ultimate reality as God is to think of God in a way that is somewhat foreign to most of us, since we tend to want to personify God, but it is in keeping with Eastern religious thinking as recorded in one of the Hindu scriptures, the Bhagavad Gita. [2]

The Bhagavad-Gita (or Song of the Lord) is a philosophical text of some seven hundred verses which occurs in the sixth book of the Mahabharata, an epic narrative of the battle between good and evil. The Gita, as it is called, tells the story of Arjuna, the third son of King Pandu, and his brother-in-law, Krishna, who was the king of a neighbouring country but who had volunteered to act as Arjuna's charioteer during the great war. On the eve of battle, Arjuna, seeing his kinsman ready to fight him, is filled with remorse at the thought of killing his relatives to gain a kingdom, and he turns to his charioteer for advice. It is Lord Krishna's advice concerning moral and religious values and man's relation to God that forms the text of the Bhagavad-Gita.

In the Bhagavad-Gita, Arjuna, having come to realize that Krishna is an avatar or incarnation of God, asks him, "Lord, which of your devotees are better versed in devotion, those who worship your image or those who worship you as the formless spirit?" Krishna replies that he prefers those who worship his image, *since it is difficult for ordinary mortals to worship Brahman as formless spirit*, which is why Hindus worship so many different images of God, each one being one aspect of that eternal Spirit.

Now, the Hindu philosophy/religion, Advaita Vedanta, which is founded on the Vedas, the earliest Hindu scriptures, speaks only about non-duality. In fact, "Advaita" means non-dual. Unfortunately, the huge majority of people seem to know nothing about even the possibility of non-duality. The reason for that is simple. In the West, for example, neutralization of the polarities in one's life was a secret for many centuries, known only to a relatively few students of the Kabbalah, the Tarot, a few Middle Ages alchemists, and 19th century occultism.

Western psychological science has only walked around the periphery of this same issue in that discipline known as Neuro-Linguistic Programming (NLP) for example. NLP is concerned with how we construct reality from sensory experience and the language through which we give it structure. Using NLP, it is relatively easy to influence a person's "reality," giving him or her greater choices about how to think about his or her experiences and, hence, what to feel and what to do. NLP teaches that it is necessary to accept the negatives of life along with the positives but, to the best of my knowledge, it has never really addressed the issue of duality itself.

Now, however, along comes someone who tackles the problem of duality head on. His name if Zivorad Slavinski, and he comes from Yugoslavia; and he has been teaching people how to quickly neutralize their Primordial Polarities – the main duality that governs an individual's life, so that they are free from the most fundamental, unconscious and compulsive problems of life. I had an opportunity to take a week-long workshop that he gave in Ontario, and I would like to tell you a bit about some of that experience.

According to Slavinski, there are two fundamental possibilities for us as conscious human beings: dualistic consciousness and unified consciousness. The majority of human beings live predominantly on the dualistic plane. This means that we see, perceive, and experience everything in opposites. Everything is always "either/or," good or bad, destroying or creating, advancing or retreating, freedom or slavery, love or freedom, life or death. This is what is known as Aristotelian thinking, and it is our heritage from the Greco-Roman background that underlies much of Western language and thought, particularly religious thought.

A few years ago, Slavinski created a process that he called Psycho Energetic Aura Technology (PEAT). On its first level, which he called Shallow Processing, PEAT has a lot of similarities with other systems of Energy Psychology, as pioneered by Roger Callahan. Its essential differences start with its second level — Deep Processing.

In PEAT Shallow Processing, you are aiming to resolve some relatively recent problem of thinking or feeling. In PEAT Deep Processing, on the other hand, you are not after diminishing immediate discomfort; essentially, you don't care about it. You are after the deepest cause of a problem. In PEAT Deep Processing, you start with a problem and you uncover one of its aspect after another on a chain leading to its deepest cause (or if you prefer, its highest cause). This process typically takes anywhere from 15 minutes to two hours, with the average being 30-50 minutes. When you get to the fundamental cause, the problem vanishes. The fundamental cause, as it turns out, is always the person's Primordial Polarities.

Slavinski offered no definite theory about how Primordial Polarities come into being, but he does offer the following thoughts: When a Spiritual Being for the first time enters from the Unmanifested Universe (Void, Sunyata, Tao) to this universe of matter, energy, time and space, that Spiritual Being posts two energetic pillars at its entrance, his/her first Yin and Yang. They define that Being's playground and, from that moment on, that Being plays his/her fundamental game of life between them. Be that as it may...

An individual's Primordial Polarities are the highest goals he or she wants to attain again and again. They are his or her most powerful attractors. But both the main characteristic and the main problem of this fundamental game of life is that it is unconscious and compulsive: in endless situations of life, the individual oscillates unconsciously and compulsively between his/her Primordial Polarities. These are not fixed values; they are like more like an alternating electric current. For a period of time, one Polarity seems to be the positive goal (the individual strives with all his or her power to attain it) and the other Polarity is negative (and he or she does his or her best to avoid it). But after some time their values change. Now, the previously avoided Polarity is sought and the previously sought polarity is avoided. And over time, they continue to switch back and forth.

What is most important for Spiritual development, and for everyday life as well, is that one can't solve the most fundamental problem in life until one attains Neutralization of his or her Primordial Polarities. According to Slavinski, you can de-stimulate that problem for a short time through practicing different spiritual disciplines, but sooner or latter it gets restimulated again. When one addresses it with PEAT Deep Processing, however, one sees his or her previous life as a series of compulsive and unconscious oscillations from one Primordial Polarity to another. After their Neutralization, the individual is welcome to continue to play the same fundamental game but, if he chooses to do so, now he or she will be playing it consciously and freely; and in Slavinski's opinion, it is only after neutralizing one's Primordial Polarities that one can begin to actually choose. Of course, Neutralization doesn't solve all your problems, just the most fundamental one. There are many others problems based on dualities, but they will be solved much easier and quicker with the same Deep PEAT process.

This Deep PEAT process is extremely straightforward. Here is a shortened version of it:

You simply start with affirmation of where you are (e.g., "Even though I am separated from God, I love and accept myself and my separation from God."), close you eyes and become aware of whatever comes to you (*as image, feeling, sensation and/or thought*), let go of the original problem, and repeat the process starting from that image, feeling, sensation or thought.

When or if you reach the beginning perception of polarization within that experience, deal with both poles as a set: first one, then the other, then both.

Follow the chain of experience until you reach peace or until you reach neutralization.

Check within yourself to see if there is any opposition to this outcome and, if so, process it as before.

Check to see if there is any possibility of the original issue returning against your will at any time in the future and, if so, process as before.

Forgive yourself (and anyone else who may have contributed to the original issue, including God).

Finally, allow God's love to enter your entire being, like a light shining down from above.

A variation of the above starts with some chosen duality and proceeds to unity as follows:

Start with affirmation of where you are (e.g., "Even though I am separated from God, I love and accept myself and my separation from God."), close your eyes and become aware of whatever comes to you (as image, feeling, sensation and/or thought). Open your eyes and share that experience with someone.

Repeat that process with the other pole of that duality (i.e., "Even though I am not separated from God, I love and accept myself and the fact that I am not separated from God."), close your eyes and become aware of whatever comes to you (as image, feeling, sensation and/or thought). Open your eyes and share that experience with someone.

Rapidly switch back and forth between these two polarities until your experience of them is no longer different, i.e., until you have the experience that that particular polarity has been neutralized, that it is, in reality, a unity. In the case of separation from God, I would expect that the final *experience* – and remember that what we are dealing with here is the experience rather than the construction of reality – would be one of there being no difference between being separated from God and being not separated from God. And from that moment on, you will always have had the experience, even if only for a moment, of unity with God.

Endnotes for Chapter 12

<u>1</u>: from the Book of Mormon

[2 Ne 1:81] For it must needs be, that there is an opposition in all things.

[2 Ne 1:82] If not so, my first born in the wilderness, righteousness could not be brought to pass; neither wickedness; neither holiness nor misery; neither good nor bad.

[2 Ne 1:83] Wherefore, all things must needs be a compound in one;

[2 Ne 1:84] Wherefore, if it should be one body, it must needs remain as dead, having no life, neither death nor corruption, nor incorruption, happiness nor misery, neither sense nor insensibility.

[2 Ne 1:85] Wherefore, it must needs have been created for a thing of naught;

[2 Ne 1:86] Wherefore, there would have been no purpose in the end of its creation.

[2 Ne 1:87] Wherefore, this thing must needs destroy the wisdom of God, and his eternal purposes; and also, the power, and the mercy, and the justice of God.

[2 Ne 1:88] And if ye shall say there is no law, ye shall also say there is no sin.

[2 Ne 1:89] And if ye shall say there is no sin, ye shall also say there is no righteousness.

[2 Ne 1:90] And if there be no righteousness, there be no happiness.

[2 Ne 1:91] And if there be no righteousness nor happiness, there be no punishment nor misery.

[2 Ne 1:92] And if these things are not, there is no God.

[2 Ne 1:93] And if there is no God, we are not, neither the earth, for there could have been no creation of things, neither to act nor to be acted upon; wherefore, all things must have vanished away.

[2 Ne 1:94] And now, my son, I speak unto you these things, for your profit and learning:

[2 Ne 1:95] For there is a God, and he hath created all things, both the heavens and the earth, and all things that in them is;

[2 Ne 1:96] Both things to act, and things to be acted upon;

[2 Ne 1:97] And to bring about his eternal purposes in the end of man, after he had created our first parents, and the beasts of the field and the fowls of the air, and in fine, all things which are created, it must needs be that there was an opposition;

[2 Ne 1:98] Even the forbidden fruit in opposition to the tree of life; the one being sweet and the other bitter;

[2 Ne 1:99] Wherefore, the Lord God gave unto man, that he should act for himself.

[2 Ne 1:100] Wherefore, man could not act for himself, save it should be that he was enticed by the one or the other.

[2 Ne 1:101] And I, Lehi, according to the things which I have read, must needs suppose that an angel of God, according to that which is written, had fallen from heaven;

[2 Ne 1:102] Wherefore he became a devil, having sought that which was evil before God.

[2 Ne 1:103] And because he had fallen from heaven, and had become miserable for ever, he sought also the misery of all mankind.

[2 Ne 1:104] Wherefore, he said, unto Eve, yea, even that old serpent, who is the devil, who is the father of all lies; wherefore he said, Partake of the forbidden fruit, and ye shall not die, but ye shall be as God, knowing good and evil.

[2 Ne 1:105] And after Adam and Eve had partaken of the forbidden fruit, they were driven out of the garden of Eden, to till the earth.

[2 Ne 1:106] And they have brought forth children; yea, even the family of all the earth.

[2 Ne 1:107] And the days of the children of men were prolonged, according to the will of God, that they might repent while in the flesh;

[2 Ne 1:108] Wherefore, their state became a state of probation, and their time was lengthened, according to the commandments which the Lord God gave unto the children of men.

[2 Ne 1:109] For he gave commandment that all men must repent;

[2 Ne 1:110] For he shewed unto all men that they were lost, because of the transgression of their parents.

[2 Ne 1:111] And now, behold, if Adam had not transgressed, he would not have fallen; but he would have remained in the garden of Eden.

[2 Ne 1:112] And all things which were created, must have remained in the same state which they were, after they were created; and they must have remained for ever, and had no end.

[2 Ne 1:113] And they would have had no children; wherefore, they would have remained in a state of innocence, having no joy, for they knew no misery; doing no good, for they knew no sin.

[2 Ne 1:114] But behold, all things have been done in the wisdom of him who knoweth all things.

[2 Ne 1:115] Adam fell, that men might be; and men are, that they might have joy.

[2 Ne 1:116] And the Messiah cometh in the fullness of time, that he may redeem the children of men from the fall.

[2 Ne 1:117] And because that they are redeemed from the fall, they have become free for ever, knowing good from evil;

[2 Ne 1:118] To act for themselves, and not to be acted upon, save it be by the punishment of the Lord, at the great and last day, according to the commandments which God hath given.

[2 Ne 1:119] Wherefore, men are free according to the flesh; and all things are given them which are expedient unto man.

2: Unlike other major religions, Hinduism has no historical founder, and it has many holy books, not just one. The earliest of these scriptures, the Vedas, date from some time after 1500 B.C. The next set of Hindu scriptures to be developed were the Upanishads, so named ("Upa-ni-shada" meaning "sitting near") because they were originally tutorials given to select pupils who sat near their teachers to hear the sacred teachings. Important because of their philosophical teachings, they have survived in their present form since about 200 B.C.E.

They contain the idea that there is a one-ness of all things throughout the created universe, that the individual soul (atman) and the universal soul (Brahman), the "One God" of Hinduism, are the same; that the visible world is an illusion (maya) but that Brahman is eternal, limitless, and omnipresent; that the individual soul is without beginning nor end but exists through a cycle of successive births and deaths (samsara); that the total effect of actions (karma) decides the next existence of the soul; and that the soul is capable of achieving freedom from its cycle of successive births and deaths and becoming (or becoming one with) Brahman through selfless action ("When all attachment arising from desires is destroyed, man's mortality ends, and only then does atman reach Brahman"). Brahman is without form, but Hindus are free to imagine this Supreme Spirit in any way that is meaningful to them, and they have done so in terms of its various aspects. The first major aspect of Brahman being Brahma (corresponding to the Vedic deity Prajapati), who created and continues to create the world.

These earliest Hindu scriptures are called shruti (or heard) texts, and are considered to be not of human origin, for they are believed to have been revealed by Brahman to certain inspired wise men of old.

The next set of Hindu scriptures, which were composed from 500 B.C.E. onwards, are called smriti (or remembered) texts. Based on tradition, this smriti literature is considered to be valid for all devout Hindus insofar as it does not contradict the shruti texts which, as a direct revelation from God, retain supreme authority.

Prominent among the smriti texts are the great Hindu epics, the Mahabharata and the Ramayana. The Mahabharata, which was composed over a period of many hundreds of years, probably beginning about four hundred B.C.E., contains 100,000 verses in eighteen books, around the central narrative of which are woven many stories with a moral message. The central story of the Mahabharata, contained in a section of the Mahabharata known as the Bhagavad-Gita, is the story of the battle between good and evil, as represented by a war between the Kuru princes and their cousins, the five sons of King Pandu, over right of succession to the throne.

CHAPTER 13

A Brief History of How Bad
Behaviour Evolved into Illness

Alexander T. Polgar, Ph.D. RSW

The impetus, indeed the compulsion, for this paper stems from what is happening globally. Today, most bad behaviour is being promoted as an illness to which the offender succumbs, albeit for reasons unspecified. Simultaneously, people in authority are promoting the power, credibility, and influence of biologically-based psychiatry. This messaging comes from professionals of all kinds, including those involved in health and human services, criminal justice, politics, business and industry, the media, and research.

As an illness, the treatment of criminal behaviour would, of course, come under the jurisdiction of physicians specializing in psychiatry or those working under their auspices. Unfortunately, however, since there is no organic evidence in support of medicalizing bad behaviour of any sort, including the criminal kind, the medical model does not apply.

Similarly, reintegrating 'cured' criminals, who became estranged from their communities during their period of 'illness', reflects a continuation of applying the medical model to a non-medical problem. In contrast, there is, in fact, a plethora of research-based literature in support of the view to be presented which, to borrow an excellent phrase, is viewed as an inconvenient truth and as such subjected to the worst kind of disdain – being ignored.

The goal of this essay is to draw attention to this inconvenient truth by chronicling how we got to where we are. The hope is that exposing the medicalization of bad behaviour will draw attention to the efforts of many others, a good sampling of which is provided in the reference section of this essay. The hope also is that this alternative perspective will be sufficiently disturbing to cause well-intentioned, good people to familiarize themselves with at least a few publications that argue against the medicalization of deviance and, indeed, the medicalization of life's daily trials and tribulations.

While this essay may sound critical of the profession of psychiatry, it is not intended as criticism of individual psychiatrists themselves but, rather, as criticism of the state of affairs in which society as a whole is abdicating its responsibility for "bad" behaviour. [16]

What follows is an effort to untangle a convoluted evolution of thought concerning physical sickness, madness, and criminal behaviour. At various times in history, the three have been viewed as either intricately related, or as separate manifestations of how humans can and should behave. For the most part, the content constitutes an effort at summarizing the works of some of the best who have critically examined the topic (Davies, 2013; Gotzsche, 2015; Moncrieff, 2009; Breggin, 2008; Whitaker and Cosgrove, 2015; Conrad and Schneider, 1992; Read, Mosher and Bentall, 2004). It is hoped that delivering this message to a new audience will expand the discussion on understanding and addressing what lies at the roots of criminality, and indeed of bad behaviour in general, and why society

---

16 There are, of course, others who are less critical of psychiatry and its Diagnostic and Statistical Manual of Mental Disorders, while acknowledging that it does have some, albeit very limited, value (see Zur & Nordmasken, 2015). The lengthy history of addressing 'mental illness' has been chronicled by others, most notably Foerschner (2010), who also provides a very useful list of references for those who wish to know more.

has chosen to concentrate its collective efforts on criminality being characterized bio-medically.[17]

Unfortunately, in spite of best efforts, language can and is used imprecisely. Concepts are wrongly used interchangeably and the difference between a disorder and an illness is poorly defined. For the purposes of this essay illness is defined as an organic process (e.g., infection) that is manifested by symptoms (e.g., fever). Disorder, dysfunctionality, madness, lunacy, etc. are all ways of labeling certain types of behaviour, including what people say. As will be discussed, the behaviours labeled as mad seldom have an organic base but nevertheless are characterized to be illness and, as such, falling within the realm of medical treatment. By so doing, social responsibility is abdicated, with the result that a cultural paradigm is rapidly emerging ratifying the medical model explanation of most bad behaviours.

HISTORY OF THOUGHT

Since the beginning of time, people have been driven to explain what they observe in their environment, including the behaviour of others. The Norwegian philosopher Jostein Gaarder (1994) in his seminal book, *Sophie's World*, does an excellent job of chronicling the evolution of thought in this regard through the centuries. Of the greatest interest is how people thought about aberrant behaviours, whether they encountered a physical malady or strange behaviour, often referred to as madness.

To illustrate, the 2000 BCE Mesopotamian worldview was that evil demons are responsible for physical ailments and the way to recovery was through divine intervention of the gods. In time,

---

17 To be consistent with the theme of this essay the words 'mental illness' are avoided as much as possible. Instead, the concepts of 'madness' and/or 'misbehaviour' are used in order to emphasize the premise that, almost always with mental disturbance, there is no condition that by definition must has an organic base.

however, supernatural explanations were replaced with observation and reason and, in the medical field, priests were gradually replaced by physicians. The most famous of all physicians was Hippocrates (460-377 B.C.E.) who was also the first to postulate the 'medical model' of madness. Hippocrates then, as do psychiatrists now, believed that emotional and mental problems are illnesses and, like all illnesses, arose out of disturbed organic processes. In spite of his focus on natural causes, however, the benefits of intervention based on the reasoning of the time was not sufficiently productive to prevent a return during the Middle Ages to viewing madness as rooted in the supernatural.

When Christianity was made the official religion of the Roman people and church and state became one in the fourth century, views about madness returned to old religious themes. At first, people believed to be possessed by Satan and/or one or other of his demons were not held responsible. The treatment of choice was exorcism directed at the expulsion of evil from the possessed. Later, with the breakdown of feudal structures, the need for scapegoats arose. This drastically changed the view of madness to badness, holding people responsible for their actions and who and whatever possessed them. For example, the 1486 witch-hunting manual of Malleus Maleficarum (Kraemer and Sprenger 1941) postulated that witches deliberately invited Satan into their lives. The obvious solution, therefore, was to destroy the host.

The Renaissance in Europe brought with it a renewed interest in ancient Greek medical approach to understanding both illness and madness. However, this move towards a therapeutic view and cure of mad or bad behaviour developed slowly. In Colonial America, change in perception and choice of intervention were even slower, perhaps due to the fact that at the time in the United States of America, there were no medical schools and very few physicians.

THE EMERGENCE OF PSYCHIATRY

By the beginning of the 18th Century, so-called lunatics, imbeciles, and morons were increasingly segregated into special institutions, the precursors to the public asylums that developed a century later. Since they were not medical institutions, the judgment of a magistrate was sufficient to send away and segregate a troublesome person. However, the American Medical Association was established in 1847 for the explicit purpose of promoting scientific and ethical medicine, its goal being to put an end to what was considered to be medical quackery. The role of physicians in dealing with strangely behaved people was at first minimal. Harmless mad people were tolerated and allowed to roam freely as long as they caused little or no trouble. In time, a physician's certificate became sufficient for commitment of someone deemed undesirable to asylums, sanatoriums/sanitariums, or what were more colloquially known as madhouses. This heralded the physicians' role as custodians of madhouses and de facto authorities on madness – authorities not because of their useful or curative treatments, but because of their willingness to be the guardians or keepers of the inept. In England, because they were better organized than other professions, physicians were successful at convincing the British Parliament to have their authority officially legislated as the dominant one.

At first, these medical directors of asylums viewed insanity as a biological disease of the brain that was 'socially caused' or precipitated by social factors. They believed that insanity was a disease of civilization and that anyone could succumb to it. Since the source of madness or bad behaviour resided in society, rather than the individual, then society, they believed, had a responsibility for these people. Moreover, given the environmental causation view, it was reasonable for them to also believe that insanity was curable. Logically, the cure required removing the afflicted from conditions that were 'making them insane', putting them in a utopian-like setting, and implementing what was then commonly referred to as moral treatment. Unfortunately, this humanistic approach was time consuming and labour intensive, and it was abandoned as admission rates to institutions swelled. While insanity or bad behaviour continued to be viewed by physicians and by the medical superintendents of asylums as a biological disease of the brain, they no longer subscribed to it being caused by social factors – although it is noteworthy that no alternative causal factors postulated.

As most asylums reverted to custodial care of internees and the use of restraints to subdue and control them, the search for environmental causes of misbehaviur was more-or-less abandoned, with both medical directors of state institutions and legislators arguing that institutionalizing certain types of badly behaved people was a better strategy than sentencing them to jail. By the mid 19th Century, most asylums were largely custodial enterprises with medical directors serving as gatekeepers and guardians, and by default the medical directors morphed into being the authority on insanity. This elevation of their status legitimized their role and, in 1884, the medical directors of thirteen insane asylums seized the opportunity, created the Association of Medical Superintendents of American Institutions for the Insane. Almost four decades later, in 1921, this name was changed to the American Psychiatric Association (APA).

A HOUSE DIVIDED

While the methods by which people deemed to be mentally ill (strangely behaved) were treated in the asylums changed from moral to custodial, a significant difference persisted among the APA members. Some continued to embrace the socially caused views about madness while others insisted on a purely biological source of affliction. Sigmund Freud's five lectures in 1909 at Clark University in Worcester Massachusetts significantly shifted the competing views in favour of social factors. He postulated that human inner conflicts were precipitated by an amalgamation of biogenetic drives and sociocultural forces evolving from parental contact/conflict and early life experiences. Subsequently, psychoanalysts became the elite of the APA and sought to create a medical monopoly by choosing to train only physicians to be analysts. This monopoly was contrary to Freud's vision and he spoke out against it several times. More recently, Scottish psychiatrist R. D. Laing (1965) had a similar view to Freud, advancing the view that madness in people is a function of an oppressive social milieu. American psychiatrist Thomas Szasz (1970) added that mental illness, in his estimation, is a form of socially deviant behaviour expressed by people who have problems living in the socially constructed realities foisted upon them.

THE SLOW BUT STEADY EMERGENCE OF BIOLOGICAL PSYCHIATRY

The first scientifically supported evidence for biologically-based madness had actually appeared in 1822 when 'general paresis', with its muscular and nerve damage, was linked to third-stage syphilis. If there is one biological cause of madness, it was argued that there must be others and that it was only a matter of time before those other biological causes were discovered. No other biological markers were found, but belief in their existence persisted. And simply put, that belief was sufficient to justify various extreme methods of physical and pharmacological interventions. Insulin shock therapy, ice baths, electroconvulsive therapy (ECT), and a sundry collection of lobotomies, of which some fifty thousand were performed in the USA, are the most familiar examples.

As these extreme forms of intervention fell into disrepute (save for ECT), four significant factors created the perfect storm that has shaped contemporary psychiatry (Whitaker and Cosgrove, 2015; Moncrieff, 2009; and Davies, 2013). The first factor was a significant advancement in pharmacology made in 1952, which was the first ever synthesis of chlorpromazine achieved by French chemists. This substance did not sedate in the traditional sense but allowed people to function better, even to improve their ability to participate in psychotherapy. The second factor had to do with the guild interest of psychiatry – in the 1950's, 60's and 70's, competition was significant from psychology, social work, non-physician psychoanalysts, and other trained counselors and therapists. The third factor had to do with psychiatry's stature in the medical profession – while psychiatrists were professing the biological basis of madness, the lack of physical evidence was starting to bring into question the claims being made. The fourth factor had to do with psychiatry's quest to emulate physical medicine's diagnostic and curative advances. However, instead of discovering and labelling the organic basis of problems, as was and is the practice in physical medicine, in the absence of empirical evidence and in support of biological theories of madness, psychiatry began and continues to (1) name disorders and to (2) detail their various symptoms. These four factors served to get psychiatry's diagnostic house in order and partner with pharmaceutical industries in pursuit of their mutually beneficial interests.

It is noteworthy that the first American text on mental disorders was written by Benjamin Rush in 1812. He advanced the view that madness is 'seated in the blood vessels' and described twenty-two distinct manifestations, twenty of which he postulated to have a biological base and two without an organic cause. The next effort to create diagnostic categories did not occur until well over a hundred years later.

In 1952, the first Diagnostic and Statistical Manual of Mental Disorders (DSM) was published. It was a relatively modest effort of 130 pages, the authors of which disproportionately represented psychoanalytically trained practitioners. The next version of the DSM, published in 1968, was similarly authored. However, concerns over reliability and validity of diagnoses and the absence of robust data in support of talk therapy shifted the focus of the DSM III Task Force, whose members once again embraced Emil Kraepelin's (1913) and Eugene Bleuler's (1911) conceptualization of schizophrenia and its causes, an underlying organic disease process – a view which, in the early 1900's, had saved psychiatry from complete obscurity (Read, 2004).

Of the four factors, the greatest role arguably was played by a pharmaceutical industry that saw a lucrative and relatively untapped market. Initially, drugs were seen as little more than soothing tonics, but by the 1970's they became aggressively marketed as medical cures capable of targeting and alleviating discrete diseases of the mind. Perhaps not surprising, the number of 'diagnosable' mental illnesses grew with each revision of the DSM. The most current edition is DSM-5, which has 947 pages and a vigorously contested number of disorders. Some believe the number of disorders and their sub-classifications are so vast as to apply to every child and adult on this planet (see for example Davies, 2013; Whitaker and Cosgrove, 2015). Instead of seeing this as a problem, the APA contends that the expansion, dissection, and elaboration of disorders is consistent with its public mission of diagnosing and effectively treating previously unrecognized mental illnesses. With this increase in the number of people diagnosable with a psychiatric disorder also comes a significant increase in the marketing and sale of psychotropic drugs. More importantly, the surge in the number of mental disorders also heralded psychiatry's influence over North American society. Indeed, psychiatry could easily claim to being the most influential medical discipline in North America as it reshapes society and what is considered to be a normal way of life.

PSYCHIATRIC IMPERIALISM

Alarmingly, this Western medicalization of everyday problems and the purported benefits of psychotropic drugs is being successfully exported globally. In just two years, through this mutually beneficial partnership, the global sale of psychotropic drugs grew to over 6 billion dollars (Whitaker and Cosgrove 2015). This trend shows no signs of abating despite evidence that prior to the emerging globalization of biological psychiatry people in developing countries with similar issues recovered at a far better rate than those in the developed countries. Davies (2013) identifies a well-orchestrated campaign launched in the

2000's that has successfully infiltrated foreign markets in Asia, South America, and Eastern Europe. This pharmaceutical industry and biological psychiatry campaign successfully recast existing regional/cultural complaints and conditions into DSM diagnostic categories. Distress and angst, which is a normal part of life, became illnesses that could be 'cured' by employing regimens founded on readily available psychotropic drugs.

The robust efforts of pharmaceutical companies and the guild of psychiatrists are aided by the World Health Organization (WHO) which, in 2001, stated that by 2020 the second leading health problem globally, after heart disease, would be clinically diagnosable depression. The solution to this looming epidemic, the report said, is making Western psychotropic drugs more widely available – if this was truly a solution then withholding it from other nations would simply be wrong. However, good objective science reveals that anti-depressants work no better than placebos for the majority of people (Moncreiff 2009).

To reiterate an earlier point, the process by which biological psychiatry and the pharmaceutical industry are expanding their influence is very much an informal one. There is no well-defined social policy in any country that sanctions the social control the two are inflicting on anyone who comes within their grasp. While the Food and Drug Administration (FDA) is an arms-length entity of government, it does not set policy or sanction specific societal/cultural perspectives about what constitutes an illness or is simply bad behaviour. What it does is to set scientific criteria for the approval of medications for people. The scientific standards applied by the FDA are only as good as the information it is provided by researchers. When scrutinized closely some alarming facts are revealed about the biases of academic researchers funded by the pharmacological industry. This has been especially true about the testing and introduction of psychotropic drugs (Whitaker and Cosgrove 2015).

The DSM's reliability and validity are and have always been contested by serious scholars (See for example, Kaplan, 1995) and have certainly not been formerly accepted as the means by which to shape any culture's interpretation or the meaning ascribed to its population's way of experiencing life. Nevertheless, according to the vastly elaborated DSM-5, virtually all negative human experiences can be classified as illness. As such, all 'illnesses' listed are within the domain of medicine, specifically the specialty of psychiatry, and since psychiatry's primary mode of understanding pathology is biochemically-based, their primary mode of intervention is psychopharmacological.

It is noteworthy, at this juncture, that other professional helping disciplines have cashed in on psychiatry's approach and influence. In many jurisdictions, psychologists are authorized to make diagnoses using the DSM. In fewer jurisdictions, social workers also are authorized to do so. Reliability and validity be damned. Furthermore, since 1984, there has been in the USA an ongoing debate regarding the right of non-physicians to prescribe psychotropic medication. Of course psychiatrists, through the APA, vehemently object to this incursion on their terrain and on this lucrative aspect of providing mental health services (Long 2005). In spite of their objection, however, two states, New Mexico and Louisiana have granted this privilege to psychologists. Thirty one other states have assembled task forces to lobby their legislatures to enact similar legislation. It would not be unreasonable to speculate that eventually all the states will follow suit.

WHO IS RESPONSIBLE

It would be grossly unjust to blame individual medical practitioners for the rapidly expanding influence of psychiatry. After all, practitioners who prescribe psychotropic drugs only know what they are taught, are socialized into throughout their training, and subsequently told by their trusted academic colleagues at conferences – as well as what they read in equally trusted peer reviewed journals. For these reasons, Whitaker and Cosgrove (2015), in their analysis of psychiatry's evolving institutional corruption, are sympathetic to best-intentioned psychiatrists and prescribing physicians. Both "have been misled" and as such have reason to feel betrayed by their own discipline.

Because well-intentioned medical practitioners have been systematically misled by guild and pharmaceutical interests, they also are ill prepared to provide information that will enable a patient to make an informed consent to treatment. This contravenes the Nuremberg Code that was explicitly crafted in response to the atrocious experiments on prisoners conducted by Nazi physicians. This legal requirement imposes a principled moral standard on all medical specialists, in this case the APA which governs the practice of psychiatry, including commissioning and publishing the ever expanding DSM. Moreover, it is the APA that provides individual physicians and psychiatrists with the information that is to be disclosed. Even an absence of knowledge is important to patients' consideration of the therapeutic options and should be shared with them. Because the prescribing physician is misled, patients are told that they have a known pathology, when there is no scientific reason to support that assertion. Clearly then, the patient cannot give 'informed consent' to the prescribed treatment.

This dissemination of misinformation is precisely what has been happening for the past 35 years or more. The APA and the larger institution of psychiatry (the guild), in collaboration with pharmaceutical industries, willfully promoted the 'understanding' that mental disorders are caused by a chemical and/or neurological imbalance in the brain and that psychiatric drugs help fix the imbalance just like 'insulin fixes the problem of diabetes'.

It is noteworthy at this juncture that, in 1999, the APA, in its Textbook of Psychiatry (Hales, 1999), acknowledged that the chemical imbalance theory of mental disorders has never been proven to be true. However, it was not until 2011 that representatives of mainstream psychiatry began admitting that fact to the public. The editor of the Psychiatric Times at the time blogged that the 'chemical imbalance' theory was a malicious caricature of psychiatry created by its critics and certainly not what the discipline has subscribed to for over 30 years. If this is truly the case, it is unfortunate that most medical practitioners have not received this information as a formal notification. Nevertheless, undeterred by the failure to prove the biochemical imbalance explanation, psychiatry is now pursuing the neurological and brain structure theories of madness, also in spite of the absence of good science in support of these theories.

PSYCHIATRY AND CRIME

As with madness, the definition of deviance has changed over the centuries from religious and moral to medical conceptualizations. Only recently has the importance of how deviance is defined been appreciated, as the extent to which the 'medical model' based on organic processes has become the answer to contemporary social problems of people behaving badly. Conrad and Schneider (1992) chronicle the history of the changes as well as the folly of applying the medical model to a behaviour problem. The corollary to medicalizing a social problem is that the remediation of it becomes the purview of the medical profession, specifically psychiatry. As psychiatry has been shaping the contemporary view of mental illness, the profession also has been shaping how deviance is conceptualized and consequently why it is treated pharmacologically. This was a natural extension of psychiatry's influence. It was a relatively easy task for the discipline to transform badness to sickness, as so eloquently described also by Conrad and Schneider (1992).

Many consider Cesare Lombroso, an Italian physician who practiced in the late 1800s, to be the father of scientific criminology (Montclair 1972). He advanced the theory that criminals, because of their physical appearance, are a biological throwback to primitive people. Similar theories about appearances can be traced back to Aristotle and include ideas about the shape and contour of the skull. Currently, the medicalization of problematic behaviour of the criminal type has gained tremendous public and governmental support for two broad categories of reason. First, it is a convenient explanation with which to abdicate social and familial responsibility. Second, psychiatry has positioned itself on a prestigious mantel, under which to rationalize a biological as opposed to a social model of criminality. Social control with sedation is a far more appealing method than the moral treatment of the past and its various new forms of today. Jesse Pitts (1968 p.391), the first to write about the medicalization of criminal behaviour almost fifty years ago, predicted that conceptualizing criminal behaviour as a medical issue is "it is one of the most effective means of social control and is destined to become the main mode" of doing so.

The medicalization of criminal behaviour, however, comes at a significant social cost. First, it creates a false sense of security and places society at risk because badly behaved people are often non-compliant when it comes to following their prescribed medication regime. Second, it creates a monopoly of control by psychiatrists and, because that monopoly excludes, squeezes out, or otherwise diminishes other disciplines that could provide alternative explanations and interventions, the presence of the medical model also serves to perpetuate the problem of crime.

For example, the empirically sound theory of criminality and cognitive developmental delay advanced by Kohlberg, Scharf and Hickey (1971 and 1974) are long forgotten and one hardly hears of therapeutic communities (De Leon, 2000) through which inmates can mature morally to be responsible adult citizens. Cognitive behaviour therapy, which has been touted as best practice, gets lost in a (medical) model that is certainly insufficient for addressing a criminal's developmentally delayed worldview that is primarily focused on the immediate satisfaction of needs.

It is noteworthy that the process of medicalization of criminal behaviour, as in the case of madness, also is being achieved without any formalized social policy process. Without well-informed debate, the process continues to evolve and, out of desperation for answers and a desire to abdicate a seemingly unacceptable social responsibility, the criminal justice system is increasingly eager to turn over their problem to biological psychiatry. The belief seems to be that, if medicine can, for example, eradicate polio, it is just a matter of time before it does the same with the behaviours exhibited by criminals (who are postulated to behave badly because they are mentally ill). In reality, however, at best it can only sedate the most difficult to manage badly behaved individuals. This requires, however, a court order since the especially badly behaved also are especially noncompliant.

AN ALTERNATIVE VIEW

In the meantime, the psychosocial model of madness and criminality has never been totally abandoned. Its primary proponent was and continues to be social work, which is now being joined by some from other disciplines. Moncrieff (2009), a psychiatrist, advocates this model in her comprehensive critique of biological psychiatry. So do psychologists Duncan and Miller (2000) who believe this to be a far better approach to understanding and addressing deviant behaviour regardless of what form it takes. Not only is the social cause theory of all forms of madness and badness alive, it has been expanded to acknowledge the unique nature of each individual and is now expressed by the more current and arguably more appropriate biopsychosocial view.

The biopsychosocial view incorporates both the nature and nurture influence on each and every individual and serves to empower by informing preventative and interventional strategies. The biological component acknowledges and takes as an undeniable fact that all individuals are born with their own unique propensities or predispositions. There is no need to discover the biological or genetic markers, although many are in the process of trying to do so. The nature component of humanity is a given. The environmental activation, or not, of that biological substratum is the social component of the concept. The psycho part of the concept refers to who we are and have the potential to become, given the interaction between the two other components of the concept. From the biopsychosocial perspective, therefore, efforts are far better spent discovering what environmental conditions promote the actualization of the individual's positive human potential, and what environmental conditions curtail it or, worse, promote dysfunctionality or deviant behaviour.

Long ago we established, but seem to have forgotten, that the most significant environmental factor is the family. Outside of today's biological psychiatry, the non-genetic based intergenerational perpetuation of dysfunctionality is a very familiar one. The idea of obstructed developmental potential also is familiar, especially in explaining deviant behaviour of the criminal type. As in the past, accepting and acting on these views requires accepting familial and social responsibility for how our children develop and who they become as adults. It is much easier to blame something else (a biological mental illness) and defer to the authority of biologically-oriented psychiatrists to fix the problem, with little effort on our part other than administering psychotropic drugs. This societal tendency to relinquish responsibility is greatly aided and abetted by the guild interests of psychiatry and the monetary pursuits of the pharmacological industry.

If we accept familial and social responsibility for what our children become as adults, we then open the door to the idea of prevention. Much has been written about prevention through promotion of the human developmental potential (Polgar 2011) and the monetary and social benefits of doing so (Heckman 2015). As such, the biopsychosocial model is not only cost effective it also produces better results for everyone.

COGNITIVE DISSONANCE

Time for taking corrective action is long overdue. Before this can be done, however, it will be necessary to address the nagging problem of cognitive dissonance – specifically, the mental distress experienced by psychiatrists and prescribing physicians because their behavior is at odds with their own beliefs (which occurs at a subconscious level) and, thereby, are a formidable obstacle to overcome (Taris, 2007).

To illustrate, physicians, and indeed most of us, generally believe ourselves to be well-intentioned and good people who create just communities in which to live. We instinctively protect this self-image and, in order to do so when our self-image conflicts with realty, we develop a good dose of cognitive dissonance. For biologically-oriented psychiatrists, the conflict comes from receiving considerable monetary benefit from the pharmacological industry. For the rest of us, the conflict is that we all come from variously dysfunctional families and inadvertently perpetuate at least some of the problems inter-generationally. For the collective, the conflict is that our culture and communities fail to adequately care for (especially) the more vulnerable. For those in the business of corrections, the conflict comes from applying an irrelevant approach to addressing the problem of crime. Consequently, many seasoned correctional personnel, while talking rehabilitation, continue to use the medical terminologies of rehabilitation and reintegration. The more frequent harm from that is the systemic obliteration of that which creates the cognitive dissonance. This was the fate of moral treatment and therapeutic communities (based on the belief of social causation) *and* the practice of family therapy (based on the belief that the most influential social factor is the family).

To address this nagging problem of cognitive dissonance first requires labeling it for what it is. Second, it requires a face-saving way out. Fortunately, the provisions for both are readily available in the correctional literature written by extremely competent scholars, a sampling of which is provided in the references to this essay.

The way out does not require invention nor innovation. There is much known about conditions that create the inter-generational perpetuation of dysfunctionality, starting with failed attachment and its myriad of later life negative consequences. Since we know what conditions create problems, we also know what conditions are required for secure attachment to take place and thereby prevent the later life negative consequences. Similarly, there is much known about facilitating cognitive development and concomitant increasingly adaptive behaviours (Likona, 1983) in children as well as in adults when they become developmentally stuck. And for those so severely damaged by their social environment that their behaviour cannot be remediated, there is an abundance of psychotropic medications that psychiatry is all too willing to prescribe.

Before concluding this essay, a brief discussion of childhood trauma is warranted. The Early Years Study, authored by Frasier Mustard and Margaret McCain (1999), unequivocally establishes the first two years of life to be the critical formative years. When conditions go awry during this time of incredible rapid growth, the infant is exposed to constant stress and the cortisol hormone causing profound physical and emotional negative consequences in later life. While there is almost no disagreement with this reality, unfortunately it has made little impact on justifying a full-scale commitment to preventative measures. Instead, society remains content to rely on the classification of children to various disorders and, particularly for attentional problems, the administration of stimulant drugs such as Ritalin. When the troublesome child becomes an adolescent or adult, the stimulants usually are replaced by street drugs. None of these strategies are curative. They simply suppress temporarily the symptoms of the harm that was done during the formative years. Interventions of potential merit are those that are provided as early as possible and focus on creating new ways of relating through corrective interpersonal attachment-focused encounters (Thomas, 1997).

CONCLUSION

It has taken psychiatry over 2000 years to establish its current level of social influence. While it is rapidly spreading globally, the continued absence of biological markers for DSM-5 disorders remains a problem, and thus their status remains, especially now, markedly tenuous. Increasingly more people are receiving good education, which threatens a specialty that essentially relies on authority, not earned but granted out of a desperate search for an easy explanation and an equally easy solution. Last, but by no means least, over the past

2000 years humanity has progressed in its understanding of the world and is more capable of accepting that a bizarre response – madness or badness – to an impossible situation is thought to be adaptive for that person at that particular time. Moreover, fewer people are willing to believe that the normal mind is a calm, peaceful, and a constantly pleasant place. The DSM-5 would have us believe that anything else is pathological, but the mind is not such an organ. It is dynamic, full of a range of emotions, often troubled, sometimes content but often discontent, the center of pain, fear, pleasure, love, and disdain. It is what it means to be alive. We do ourselves an enormous disservice when we allow most of it to be defined as pathology rather than accepting that this is just the way life is.

REFERENCES

Bleuler, E. (1911). Dementia Praecox or the group of schizophrenias. New York: International University of Press.

Breggin, Peter (2008). Medication madness: The role of psychiatric drugs in cases of violence, suicide and crime. New York: St. Martin's Press.

Caplan, Paula J. (1995). They say you're crazy. How the world's most powerful psychiatrists decide who's normal. Reading, Massachusetts: Perseus Books

Conrad, Peter and Schneider, Joseph W. (1992). Deviance and medicalization: From badness to sickness. Philadelphia: Temple University Press.

Davies, James (2013). Cracked: Why psychiatry is doing more harm than good. London: Icon Books Ltd.

De Leon, George (2000). The therapeutic community. New York, New York: Spinger Publishing.

Duncan, Barry L. and Miller, Scott, D. (2000). The heroic client. San Fransciso: Joney – Bass.

Ferrell, Bridget (2015) <u>Difference in prison philosophies: The Danish Prison system vs the US Prison System</u>. Atonion Scholars Honors Program. Page 39.

Garder, Jostein (1996). <u>Sophie's world: A novel about the history of philosophy</u>. New York; Berkley Books.

Gotzsche, Peter (2015). <u>Deadly psychiatry and organized denial</u>. UK: Art People.

Hales, R./ (Ed.) (1999). <u>Textbook of psychiatry</u>. DC: American Psychiatric Press.

Heckman, James (2014). <u>Early childhood education benefits all</u>. Chicago: Bloomberg Businessweek.

Kohlberg, L., Kauffman, K., Scharf, P., Hickey, J. (1974). <u>The just community approach to corrections</u>. Harvard University Graduate School of Education: Cambridge, Massachusetts.

Kohlberg, L., Scharf, P. and Hickey, J. (1971). The justice structure of the prison: A theory and an intervention. <u>The Prison Journal</u>, Volume II, Number 2.

Kraemer, M. and Sprenger, M. ([1486] 1941). <u>Malleus Maleficorum</u> (translated by D. Summer). London: Pashkin.

Kraepelin, E (1913). Dementia Praecox. In E. Kraepelin (Ed.), <u>Psychiatrica, 8th Edn</u>. Melbourne, F.L.: Krieger.

Laing, R.D. (1965). <u>The divided self</u>. Harmondsworth: Pelican Books.

Lickona, Thomas (1983). <u>Raising good children</u>. New York: Bantam Books.

Long, James E. Jr. (2005). The debate over the prescription privilege for psychologists and the legal issues implicated. <u>National Register of Health Service Psychologists</u>, Fall Edition.

McCain, Margaret Narrie and Mustard, J. Fraiser (1999). <u>Early years study</u>. Publications Toronto: Ontario.

Moncreiff, Joanne (2009). <u>The myth of the chemical cure: A critique of psychiatric drug treatment</u>. New York: Palgrave McMillan.

Montclair, N.J. (1972). <u>Criminal man: According to the classification of Cesare Lombroso</u>. N.J.: Patterson Smith Publishing Corp..

Pitts, J. (1968). Social Control: The concept. In De Sills (Ed). International Encyclopedia of Social Sciences (Vol 14). New York: Macmillian Publishing Co.

Polgar, A. T. (2002). Because we can: Achieving the human developmental potential in five generations. Hamilton: Sandriam Publications.

Read, John, (2004). The invention of 'schizophrenia'. In J. Read, L.R. Masker, R.P. Bental (Eds.), Models of madness. London and New York: Routledge Taylor & Francis Group.

Read, John, Mosher, Loren R., Bentall, Richard (2004). Models of madness: Psychological, social and biological approaches to schizophrenia. New York: Routledge.

Szasz, T. (1970) Ideology and insanity: Essays on the psychiatric dehumanization of man. New York: Anchor Books.

Tavris, C. (2007). "Why won't they admit they're wrong? And other skeptics' mysteries". Skeptical Inquirer 31, 12-13.

Thomas, Nancy L. (2008) When love is not enough: A guide to parenting children with reactive attachment disorder. Colorado: Families By Design Inc..

Whitaker, Robert and Cosgrove, Lisa (2015). Psychiatry under the influence. New York: Palgrave MacMillan.

CPSIA information can be obtained
at www.ICGtesting.com
Printed in the USA
LVHW041931260419
615749LV00001B/178